California
Infant/Toddler
Curriculum Framework

California Department of Education
Sacramento, 2012

Publishing Information

The *California Infant/Toddler Curriculum Framework* was developed by the California Department of Education/Child Development Division (CDE/CDD). The publication was edited by John McLean, working in cooperation with Tom Cole and Lisa Duerr, Consultants, Child Development Division. It was prepared for printing by the staff of CDE Press, with the cover and interior design created by Juan D. Sanchez. The document was published by the California Department of Education, 1430 N Street, Sacramento, CA 95814-5901. It was distributed under the provisions of the Library Distribution Act and *Government Code* Section 11096.

© 2012 by the California Department of Education
All rights reserved

ISBN: 978-0-8011-1723-7

Ordering Information

Copies of this publication are available for purchase from the California Department of Education (CDE). For prices and ordering information, visit http://www.cde.ca.gov/re/pn/rc/ or call the CDE Press sales office at 1-800-995-4099.

Notice

The guidance in the *California Infant/Toddler Curriculum Framework* is not binding on local educational agencies or other entities. Except for statutes, regulations, and court decisions referenced herein, the document is exemplary, and compliance with it is not mandatory. (See *Education Code* Section 33308.5.)

Contents

A Message from the State Superintendent of Public Instruction v

Acknowledgments vi

Chapter 1: Introduction to the Framework 1
- California's Infants and Toddlers 1
- Overarching Principles 4
- Organization of the Infant/Toddler Curriculum Framework 9
- Dual-Language Development and Learning in All Domains 10
- Universal Design for Learning 11
- Program Features That Support Effective Infant/Toddler Curriculum 12
- The Infant/Toddler Learning Process: The Starting Point 12
- Curriculum Planning 19
- Reflections on Observation, Documentation, Assessment, and Planning 32
- Implementation of a Plan 44
- Endnotes 48
- Bibliography 49

Chapter 2: The California Early Learning and Development System 53
- Infant/Toddler Learning and Development Foundations 54
- Infant/Toddler Curriculum Framework 55
- Desired Results Assessment System—*Desired Results Developmental Profile (DRDP)* 56
- Program Guidelines and Other Resources 59
- Professional Development 60
- In-Depth Understanding and Planning for Children's Integrated Learning 60
- Bibliography 61

Chapter 3: Social–Emotional Development 63
- Guiding Principles 64
- Summary of the Foundations 67
- Environments and Materials 67
- Interactions 69
- Engaging Families 75
- Questions for Reflection 76
- Concluding Thoughts 77
- Map of the Foundations 78
- Teacher Resources 78
- Endnotes 79
- Bibliography 81

Chapter 4: Language Development 83
Guiding Principles 84
Summary of the Foundations 88
Environments and Materials 88
Interactions 89
Engaging Families 94
Questions for Reflection 95
Concluding Thoughts 95
Map of the Foundations 96
Teacher Resources 97
Endnotes 98
Bibliography 98

Chapter 5: Cognitive Development 101
Guiding Principles 102
Summary of the Foundations 106
Environments and Materials 107
Interactions 110
Engaging Families 116
Questions for Reflection 117
Concluding Thoughts 118
Map of the Foundations 119
Teacher Resources 120
Endnotes 120
Bibliography 121

Chapter 6: Perceptual and Motor Development 123
Guiding Principles 127
Summary of the Foundations 130
Environments and Materials 130
Interactions 132
Engaging Families 138
Questions for Reflection 139
Concluding Thoughts 140
Map of the Foundations 141
Teacher Resources 142
Endnotes 143
Bibliography 145

Appendix: Resources for Teachers of Children with Disabilities or Other Special Needs 147

A Message from the State Superintendent of Public Instruction

I am pleased to present the *California Infant/Toddler Curriculum Framework*. Infancy is a distinctive period in a child's life that calls for unique responses from adults. In the past 20 years, research has told us much about brain development, how children learn, and how best to facilitate that learning. We now know that from the moment of birth, infants are ready to learn and are able to absorb information rapidly to understand the world around them.

Created as a companion publication to the *California Infant/Toddler Learning and Development Foundations*, this framework supports caregivers as they strive to make teaching responsive and meaningful for infants and toddlers. It presents strategies and information to enrich learning and development opportunities and provides a structure that infant/toddler providers and administrators can use to make informed decisions as they plan learning environments and experiences for our youngest children. Like the infant/toddler foundations, the framework is based on current research on how infants and toddlers learn and develop in four domains: (1) social–emotional, (2) language, (3) cognitive, and (4) perceptual and motor development.

The framework emphasizes both the central role of the family in a young child's learning and development and the diversity of California's families. Attention is given to the importance of responsive, individualized care that is grounded in children's secure relationships with their parents and primary caregivers. Seen as part of a comprehensive system, the infant/toddler curriculum framework supports effective planning and the ongoing cycle of observing, documenting, reflecting, and implementing appropriate curriculum.

The *California Infant/Toddler Curriculum Framework* speaks to infant/toddler care professionals, program directors, faculty of higher education, and families. By understanding the development and learning process of infants and toddlers, early childhood professionals can effectively support early learning, program directors can create high-quality learning environments, and faculty can better prepare tomorrow's infant care teachers. Family members can better share their knowledge of their children and work as partners with caregivers to support infants' and toddlers' active exploration and learning. I hope this resource helps every adult understand how to create a strong foundation for the child's well-being and long-term success.

Tom Torlakson
TOM TORLAKSON
State Superintendent of Public Instruction

Acknowledgments

The development of the *California Infant/Toddler Curriculum Framework* involved many people. We gratefully acknowledge each of the following contributors to this publication.

Project Leader
Peter Mangione, WestEd

Panel of Experts
Marc Bornstein, National Institute of Health and Human Development
Vera Gutierrez-Clellen, San Diego State University
Jeree Pawl, Clinical Psychologist
Ross Thompson, University of California, Davis
Marlene Zepeda, California State University, Los Angeles

Writers

Chapter 1: Introduction to the Framework

J. Ronald Lally, WestEd
Mary Jane Maguire-Fong, American River College
Peter Mangione, WestEd

Chapter 2: The California Early Learning and Development System

Jenna Bilmes, WestEd
Melinda Brookshire, WestEd
Jan Davis, WestEd
Peter Mangione, WestEd
Charlotte Tilson, WestEd

Chapter 3: Social–Emotional Development

Min Chen, WestEd
Deborah Greenwald, WestEd
Janis Keyser, Cabrillo College
Peter Mangione, WestEd
Margie Perez-Sesser, Consultant
Charlotte Tilson, WestEd
Cathy Tsao, WestEd
Elita Amini Virmani, WestEd

Chapter 4: Language Development

Min Chen, WestEd
Deborah Greenwald, WestEd
Peter Mangione, WestEd
Margie Perez-Sesser, Consultant
Charlotte Tilson, WestEd
Cathy Tsao, WestEd
Elita Amini Virmani, WestEd

Chapter 5: Cognitive Development

Min Chen, WestEd
Deborah Greenwald, WestEd
Mary Jane Maguire-Fong, American River College
Peter Mangione, WestEd
Margie Perez-Sesser, Consultant
Charlotte Tilson, WestEd
Cathy Tsao, WestEd
Elita Amini Virmani, WestEd

Chapter 6: Perceptual and Motor Development

Min Chen, WestEd
Deborah Greenwald, WestEd
Peter Mangione, WestEd
Alice Nakahata, Consultant
Margie Perez-Sesser, Consultant

Charlotte Tilson, WestEd
Cathy Tsao, WestEd
Elita Amini Virmani, WestEd

Appendix: Resources for Teachers of Children with Disabilities or Other Special Needs

Kai Kaiser, WestEd

Universal Design Advisers

Linda Brault, WestEd
Kai Kaiser, WestEd

WestEd Center for Child and Family Studies—Project Staff and Advisers

Eva Gorman
J. Ronald Lally
Peter Mangione
Katie Monahan
Amy Schustz-Alvarez
Charlotte Tilson
Cathy Tsao
Sara Webb-Schmitz

California Department of Education

Lupita Cortez Alcalá, Deputy Superintendent, Instruction and Learning Support Branch
Camille Maben, Director, Child Development Division
Cecelia Fisher-Dahms, Administrator, Quality Improvement Office, Child Development Division
Tom Cole, Consultant, Child Development Division
Lisa Duerr, Consultant, Child Development Division
Mary Smithberger, Former Consultant, Child Development Division
Gwen Stephens, Former Assistant Director, Child Development Division

Focus Groups (Public Input)

Thank you to the focus-group participants who offered valuable feedback and suggestions.

Photographer

Sara Webb-Schmitz, WestEd

Photographs

Many thanks to the following programs for graciously allowing us to photograph their staff members, children, and families:

Associated Students, Inc., Children's Center, California State University, Sacramento
Associated Students, Inc., Children's Center, San Francisco State University
Blue Skies for Children
The Cameron School
Contra Costa Community College Early Learning Center
Covina Child Development Center
Little Munchkins Academy
Marin Head Start, 5th Avenue Early Head Start
Marin Head Start, Hamilton Campus
Marin Head Start, Indian Valley Campus
Marin Head Start, Meadow Park Campus
Merced College Child Development Center
Solano Community College Children's Programs
University of California, Los Angeles, Infant Development Program
Willow Street School House
Yerba Buena Gardens Child Development Center

Note: The names, titles, and affiliations of the people listed in these acknowledgments were current at the time the publication was developed.

Chapter 1
Introduction to the Framework

The purpose of the *California Infant/Toddler Curriculum Framework* is to provide early childhood professionals with a structure they can use to make informed decisions about curriculum practices. The framework is based on current research on how infants and toddlers learn and develop in four domains: social–emotional, language, cognitive, and perceptual and motor development. It presents principles for supporting early learning, a planning process, and strategies to assist infant/toddler care teachers* in their efforts to support children's learning from birth to age three.

This document presents general guidance on planning learning environments and experiences for young children. The California Department of Education (CDE) brought together leading experts in developmental theory and research, and sought input from early childhood professionals throughout California, to ensure this curriculum framework accurately reflects current research, theory, and widely accepted practices in the infant/toddler field. The framework is intended to be consistent with a broad range of curricula or specific curricular approaches. It includes a sampling of strategies for building on children's competencies and interests in four major developmental domains and describes the types of environments and materials that engage young children in learning.

The primary audience for this framework is infant/toddler care teachers (who work in centers or family child care programs) and infant/toddler program directors and supervisors. Parents, early childhood faculty in higher education, and trainers may also find the framework useful.

California's Infants and Toddlers

A fundamental consideration in planning curriculum for individual children is being responsive to the competencies, experiences, interests, and needs each child brings to the preschool classroom. California's infant/toddler population includes

---

*The term *infant/toddler care teachers* is used throughout this publication to describe early childhood professionals who work directly with young children, ages zero to three, by providing emotional and social support while also addressing the intellectual, language, and perceptual and motor development of the children. The abbreviated word *teachers* is often used in place of the longer term.

children who are culturally diverse, linguistically diverse, diverse in ability, and from diverse socioeconomic backgrounds. Partnering with families is an important strategy for being responsive to individual children and for making curriculum individually and culturally relevant.

An increasingly prominent factor in the diversity of the state's children is their early experiences with language. Language and literacy development contributes to young children's learning and long-range success in many different ways. Children who enter an infant/toddler program with emerging competence in a language other than English rely on their home language to learn. Continuing to build competence in their home language allows children to draw on all of their knowledge and skills as they continue to engage in learning.

Socioeconomic diversity is another trend that merits attention. The percentage of children living in low-income homes is high. At the same time, the benefits of high-quality care and education are more pronounced for children from low-income backgrounds than for other population subgroups. Children from diverse socioeconomic backgrounds are more likely to benefit from high-quality care and education when the curriculum is attuned to their learning strengths and needs.

Children with disabilities or other special needs are another part of California's population of young children. Children with disabilities or other special needs benefit from learning in inclusive environments with typically developing children. Studies have shown that with appropriate support and assistance, children in inclusive environments achieve more than children in segregated environments.[1]

As the following information suggests, the diversity of young children means that every infant/toddler program needs a flexible approach to curriculum in order to be responsive to all children who enter its doors.

Diversity

Compared with most other states, California has an extraordinarily diverse population of children, particularly those under the age of five. More than six million children were enrolled in California's K–12 schools in 2008–09; 49 percent were Latino/Hispanic, 27.9 percent were white, 8.4 percent were Asian, 7.3 percent were African American, and 2.7 percent were Filipino.[2] Similarly, among the 3.2 million children from birth to age five living in California during 2008, 51 percent were Latino, 30 percent were white, 10 percent were Asian, and 7 percent were African American.[3] These trends are anticipated to continue over the next several decades.

Dual-Language Learners

Data for the 2008–09 school year indicate that in California, there are more children who are dual-language learners enrolled in younger grades than in older grades.[4] In its *California Report Card 2010*, Children Now estimates that 40 percent of children in California's kindergarten classrooms are dual-language learners.[5] In an earlier report (from 2004), Children Now and Preschool California indicated that young children living in linguistically isolated homes are less likely to be enrolled in preschool programs.[6]

The broad range of languages spoken by children in the state is clearly a significant factor in developing curriculum for infants and toddlers. During the 2008–09 school year, 84.8 percent of California children in kindergarten through grade twelve who were learning English spoke Spanish, followed by Vietnamese (2.4 percent), Filipino (1.5 percent), Cantonese (1.4 percent), Hmong (1.2 percent), and Korean (1.0 percent).[7] Many families come from the same geographic regions outside the United States, but those families do not necessarily speak the same language.[8] In many infant/toddler programs, children whose families speak a different language at home may be experiencing English for the first time. It is important to support children's development of their home language as they start to learn English. Competence in two languages will allow children to become adults who can contribute to both the global economy and their local communities. Infant/toddler programs in which English is spoken can best support young children by being responsive to the children's communication in their home language as well as in English, while supporting the children's continuing development of their families' language.

Socioeconomic Status

The National Center for Children in Poverty (NCCP) documented that in 2008, approximately 45 percent of children in California under the age of six lived in a low-income family. Compared with other states, California ranks 20th in the nation for the number of children under age eighteen who are living in poverty.[9] According to the NCCP, younger children (birth to age six) are more likely to live in a low-income household.[10] Young children of immigrant parents are 20 percent more likely to live in a low-income family than children with native-born parents. Young African American, Latino, and Native American children in California are also more likely than white children to live in low-income families.[11]

Children with Special Needs

In 2008, over 77,000 children from birth to age five with identified disabili-

ties attended preschool in California.[12] This number does not include children at risk of a disability or developmental challenges. Children with disabilities represent the diversity of California's entire early childhood population and necessitate unique care and educational considerations in infant/toddler settings. Children under the age of three with identified disabilities have individualized family service plans (IFSPs) that reflect the CDE's infant/toddler learning and development foundations.

Overarching Principles

The infant/toddler curriculum framework rests on the following principles:

- The family is at the core of a young child's learning and development.
- Infant/toddler learning and development is grounded in relationships.
- Emotions drive early learning and development.
- Responsiveness to children's self-initiated exploration fosters learning.
- Individualized teaching and care benefits all children.
- Responsiveness to culture and language supports children's learning.
- Intentional teaching and care enriches children's learning experiences.
- Time for reflection and planning enhances teaching and care.

These principles have guided the development of this framework. The rationales for the principles follow.

The family is at the center of a young child's learning and development

California's infant/toddler learning and development program guidelines describe the family's influence on early learning and development in the following way:

> Family relationships have more influence on a child's learning and development than any other relationships he has. Family members know him better than anyone else. They know his usual way of approaching things, his interests, how he likes to interact, how he is comforted, and how he learns. Family members understand his strengths, and they have learned how to help him with any special needs he may have. Just as important, the child's relationships with family members shape the way he experiences relationships outside the home.[13]

In light of the family's central role in a child's early experience and development, programs need to partner with family members in all aspects of curriculum planning. Strong partnerships with families grow from respecting and valuing diverse views, expectations, goals, and understandings families have for their children. Programs demonstrate respect for families by exchanging information about their children's learning and development and sharing ideas about how to support learning at home and in the infant/toddler program. Partnerships with families extend to the community in which the families live, come together, and support one another. Building connections to the surrounding community allows a program to become known and to make use of community resources. Getting to know the community also gives teachers insights into the learning experiences and competencies that children bring to the infant/toddler setting and informs efforts to make infant/toddler care and teaching responsive and meaningful for children.

Infant/toddler learning and development is grounded in relationships

Relationships provide infants and toddlers a secure emotional base from which they can explore and learn. Much of the cognitive, language, social, and physical learning a child experiences occurs while interacting with an adult. In fact, relationships with others are at the center of young children's lives. Caring relationships with close family members provide the base for young children to engage with others, to explore with confidence, to seek support when needed, and to view interactions with others as likely to be positive and interesting. Recognizing the power of early relationships, infant/toddler care teachers and programs build strong relationships with children and families. Just as important, infant/toddler care teachers nurture the social–emotional development of young children through relationships. Research shows that healthy social–emotional development helps young children learn—for example, to sustain attention more easily, to make and maintain friendships, and to communicate needs and ideas. A climate of caring and respect that promotes nurturing relationships between children and within the community of families supports children's learning in all domains.

Emotions drive early learning and development

A child's emotional state drives early learning and greatly influences learning in other domains. The pleasure an infant experiences when receiving a positive response from a nurturing adult or when making a discovery motivates the child to continue engaging in positive interactions and exploration. For infants and toddlers, learning always has an emotional component. They are highly sensitive to the emotional cues of other people and are emotionally expressive in every situation. In light of the integral nature of emotions in early learning, adults who plan curriculum for infants and toddlers must always consider the emotional impact of the environment and experiences on the child.[14]

During the infancy period, children simultaneously exhibit both emotional vulnerability and learning competence. Infants are utterly dependent on adult nurturance for survival. They rely on adults to get their needs met and can become emotionally secure or insecure depending on the responses they receive from adults. They relate to adults as wise elders who can help them cope with difficult moments and guide them in their interactions with others. At the same time, infants and toddlers are amazingly competent. They are curious, motivated learners who actively explore the world of people and things. Infants' and toddlers' active engagement in learning propels their learning in all domains. The optimal context for their lively engagement in learning is relationships in which their competence is respected and encouraged and their emotional vulnerability is regulated through predictable, positive nurturance.

Responsiveness to children's self-initiated exploration fosters learning

Research shows that responsive care and nurturance not only promotes the development of emotional security in children, but learning and development in general. For example, when compared with young infants who receive nonresponsive care, young infants who receive consistent, appropriate, and prompt responses cry less often when they are older.[15] Being responsive to nondistress cues from children also has an impact. In a chapter titled "Caregiver Responsiveness and Cognitive Development in Infants and Toddlers: Theory and Research," published in the Program for Infant/Toddler Care (PITC) guide *Infant/Toddler Caregiving: A Guide to Cognitive Development and Learning,* Bornstein offers the following summary:

> One group of infants had mothers who, during the middle of the child's first year, were responsive to their child's nondistress signals (such as vocalization, facial expression, and movements). At thirteen months, those infants tended to show an advantage in language and play. A second group consisted of four-year-old children whose mothers had been responsive when the children were infants. Those children tended to solve problems more efficiently and scored higher on a standardized intelligence test than did their peers with less responsive mothers.[16]

Aligned with the approach recommended in this curriculum framework, the PITC provides guidance to infant/

toddler care teachers on how to create responsive relationships with infants and toddlers. In essence, observation and reflection are at the heart of being responsive to the interests and needs of infants and toddlers.

Individualized teaching and care benefits all children

Each child is unique. Infant/toddler care teachers use their understanding of each child's blend of temperament, family and cultural experiences, language experiences, personal strengths, interests, abilities, and dispositions to support the child's learning and development. Through recognizing and adapting to each child's individual development, teachers are able to offer learning experiences that are responsive, meaningful, and developmentally attuned to each child. Providing interactions, experiences, and an environment that meet the individual needs of children with disabilities or other special needs can enrich the experiences of all children in the program.* A classroom environment in which all children are supported and feel welcome creates rich learning experiences for everyone.

When children with disabilities or other special needs are included, the partnership with families is especially important. The family is the primary bridge between the preschool staff and special services the child may be receiving. The family, teacher, and other program staff members can work together and include other specialists in the preschool setting. Adapting to an individual child may mean modifying the learning environment to "increase a child's access, potential and availability for learning through thoughtful organization of materials and space."[17] Specifically designed professional support and development opportunities, as well as specialized instructional strategies, can help teachers deliver individualized education and care to meet the needs of all the children in a program.

Responsiveness to culture and language supports children's learning

Responsive infant/toddler programs create a climate of respect for each child's culture and language. Teachers and other program staff members partner and regularly communicate with family members to get to know the cultural strengths each child brings to the program. An essential part of being culturally and linguistically responsive is to value and support each child's use of home language, as "continued use and development of the child's home language will benefit the child as he or she acquires English."[18] Equally important are nurturing interactions with children and their families in which "teachers attempt, as much as possible, to learn about the history, beliefs, and practices of the children and families they serve."[19] In addition to being responsive to the cultural history, beliefs, values, ways of communicating, and practices of children and families, teachers create learning environments that include resources such as pictures, displays, and books that are culturally rich and supportive of diversity, particularly the cultures and languages of the children and families in their infant/toddler care setting.[20, 21]

---

*An additional resource for supporting your work with children with special needs is *Inclusion Works! Creating Child Care Programs That Promote Belonging for Children with Special Needs,* a publication of the California Department of Education. The book is listed in the bibliography at the end of this chapter.

Intentional teaching and care enriches children's learning experiences

Effective curriculum planning occurs when teachers are mindful of children's learning and are intentional in their efforts to support it. In *The Intentional Teacher,* a publication of the National Association for the Education of Young Children (NAEYC), Ann Epstein offers the following description:

> [T]he intentional teacher . . . acts with knowledge and purpose to ensure that young children acquire the knowledge and skills (content) they need to succeed in school and in life. Intentional teachers use their knowledge, judgment, and expertise to organize learning experiences for children; when an unexpected situation arises . . . they can recognize a teaching opportunity and are able to take advantage of it, too.[22]

With an understanding of early learning and development, the teacher supports learning in areas identified by California's infant/toddler learning and development foundations. The intentional teacher is flexible in order to accommodate differences in children's learning strengths and needs. Reflective, intentional teaching strategies include the planning of learning environments, experiences, and routines as well as spontaneous responses suggested by the moment-to-moment focus of the children.

Time for reflection and planning enhances teaching and care

Infant/toddler care teachers are professionals who serve an important role in society. In nurturing the development of infants and toddlers, teachers engage in an ongoing process of observation, documentation and assessment, reflection and planning, and implementation of strategies in order to provide individualized and small-group learning experiences. As increasing numbers of children with diverse backgrounds, including children with disabilities, participate in infant/toddler programs, collaboration, teaming, and communication are essential to extending the benefits of high-quality infant/toddler care to all children. Curriculum planning requires time for teachers to reflect on children's learning and plan strategies that foster children's progress in building knowledge and mastering skills. Infant/toddler programs that support intentional teaching and care allocate time in teachers' schedules for both individual and team reflection and planning. With appropriate support, teachers are able to grow professionally through a continuous process of learning together and exploring ways to be responsive to young children's learning interests and needs.

Organization of the Infant/Toddler Curriculum Framework

As stated previously, the infant/toddler curriculum framework builds on the California infant/toddler learning and development foundations, which describe the learning and development that infants and toddlers typically demonstrate with appropriate support in the following four domains:

- Social–Emotional Development
- Language Development, which includes Early Literacy Development
- Cognitive Development
- Perceptual and Motor Development

This introductory chapter presents the general considerations upon which the infant/toddler curriculum framework is built, including information on California's diverse infant/toddler population, overarching principles, dual-language development and learning, universal design, program features that support effective infant/toddler curriculum, how infants and toddlers learn, and curriculum planning and implementation.

Chapter 2 describes the California Early Learning and Development System, which includes the state's infant/toddler learning and development foundations, this curriculum framework, the Desired Results assessment system, the infant/toddler learning and development program guidelines, other related resources, and professional development. Each of these resources is defined, and the chapter presents an overview of how these different resources form an integrated system that promotes high-quality learning environments and experiences for infants and toddlers.

Chapters 3 through 6 focus on the four domains in the infant/toddler foundations. Each chapter covers one domain and presents guiding principles; a summary of the foundations for the domain; descriptions of environments, materials, and interactions that support learning and development in that domain; questions for reflection; and resources for teachers.

Dual-Language Development and Learning in All Domains

The progress that infants and toddlers make as they learn either one language or two languages varies greatly from child to child. Some children enter a program as young infants who rely primarily on nonverbal communication. Some children enter a program with experience in a language other than English. Other children may have some experience with English but mainly rely on their home language to communicate. And there may be older toddlers who are learning English as a second language and may be fairly sophisticated in their understanding and use of English. Infants and toddlers who are learning English while they are also developing their home-language abilities use their knowledge and skills in their first language to continue to make progress in all other domains. Children who are dual-language learners also vary greatly in the level of proficiency in their first language, which, in turn, influences their progress in English-language development.

In an integrated curriculum, the key to supporting all children is to plan learning environments and experiences based on an ongoing understanding of each child's interests, needs, and family and cultural experiences. For young children who are dual-language learners, this approach requires focused attention to each child's experiences in acquiring a second language and an understanding of how to use a child's first language to help him or her understand a second language. In applying an integrated approach, teachers take advantage of every moment to provide children with opportunities to communicate with greater understanding and skill. There are several key considerations for supporting infants and toddlers' learning of their home language and English in infant/toddler care settings, including these:

- Children who are learning English as a second language possess a

home language upon which effective support can be based.

- Children who are learning English as a second language may demonstrate language knowledge and skills in their home language before they demonstrate the same knowledge and skills in English.

- Children who are learning English as a second language may need additional support and time to engage in communication that includes English knowledge and skills; infant/toddler care teachers need to scaffold children's learning experiences and use multiple modes of communication, particularly nonverbal cues.

- In an integrated approach to curriculum in early care and education settings, an intentional focus on the process of learning English as a second language is necessary at all times.

The level of additional support and time that dual-language learners need to demonstrate the knowledge and skills described by the foundations in the social–emotional development, cognitive development, and perceptual and motor development domains will be influenced by the children's development in both their first language and English. The language the child speaks at home, as well as the amount and variety of experience the child has in the home language, will likely affect the amount and type of support the child needs.

Although focused on preschool children, the California Department of Education's DVD titled *A World Full of Language: Supporting Preschool English Learners* offers recommendations that apply to caring for infants and toddlers. In particular, this resource highlights the importance of a climate of acceptance and belonging as the starting point for giving additional support to children who are learning English as a second language. In effective programs, intentional efforts:

- focus on the children's sense of belonging and need to communicate;
- allow children to participate voluntarily;
- create opportunities for interaction and play with peers.

While learning and trying to use English, children need to feel comfortable with everyone in the infant/toddler care setting, with the use of their home language, and with nonverbal ways to express themselves.

Universal Design for Learning

This infant/toddler curriculum framework applies to all young children in California, including children with disabilities or other special needs. In some cases, children with disabilities or other special needs demonstrate their developmental progress in diverse ways. Recognizing that children follow different pathways to learning, this framework incorporates a concept known as universal design for learning.

Universal design provides for multiple means of representation, expression, and engagement.[23] *Multiple means of representation* refers to providing information in a variety of ways so the learning needs of all the children are met. *Multiple means of expression* refers to allowing children to use alternative ways to communicate or demonstrate what they know or what they are feeling. *Multiple means of engagement* refers to providing choices within the setting or program that facilitate learning by building on children's interests. The information in this curriculum framework has been worded to incorporate multiple means of representation, expression, and engagement.

Program Features That Support Effective Infant/Toddler Curriculum

The impact of curriculum is either enhanced or dampened by the context in which it is implemented. Creating a strong programmatic context for curriculum implementation is very important. Program policies set the stage for infant/toddler learning and development. Program policies that support effective infant/toddler curriculum planning and implementation include these elements:

- **Primary Care**—assigning a primary infant care teacher to each child and family
- **Small Groups**—creating small groups of children and caregivers
- **Continuity**—maintaining consistent teacher assignments and groups over time
- **Personalized Care**—responding to individual needs, abilities, and schedules
- **Cultural Continuity**—maintaining cultural consistency between home and program through dialogue and collaboration with families
- **Inclusion of Children with Special Needs**—providing appropriate accommodations and support for children with disabilities or other special needs.

More comprehensive descriptions of these recommended program policies can be found in the 2006 CDE publication *Infant/Toddler Learning and Development Program Guidelines*, a companion document to California's *Infant/Toddler Learning and Development Foundations* publication and this curriculum framework.

The Infant/Toddler Learning Process: The Starting Point

In the past 20 years, research has uncovered a vast amount of information about how young children learn and how that learning is best facilitated. Research has shown that infants are ready to learn from birth; they are able to absorb information from the sights, sounds, and scents around them, to store it, to sort it out, and to use it.[24] This information helps infants understand the world and the people around them.

Research has also shown that infants and toddlers are quite dependent on primary relationships for their physical and emotional needs to be met. Aware of this need, teachers plan their interactions with infants and toddlers to address both the vulnerability and the competence of children. In doing so, teachers simultaneously attend to the children's need for close, consistent relationships with nurturing adults and to the children's curiosity and motivation to learn.

Infant and Toddler Development and Its Facilitation

Because everything is new to infants and toddlers, and their brains are developing rapidly, infancy is a unique period of life that calls for unique responses from adults. The ways infants and toddlers think, feel, and function differ somewhat from the ways children in the developmental periods of preschool, middle childhood, and adolescence think, feel, and function. Synapse formation in different developmental areas peaks at different times from birth to age three. The National Scientific Council on the Developing Child characterizes the development during infancy in the following way:

> Because low-level circuits mature early and high-level circuits mature later, different kinds of experiences are critical at different ages for optimal brain development, a concept called *age-appropriate experience*.

Soon after birth, basic sensory, social, and emotional experiences are essential for optimizing the architecture of low-level circuits. At later ages, more sophisticated kinds of experiences are critical for shaping higher-level circuits. When adults or communities expect young children to master skills for which the necessary brain circuits have not yet been formed, they waste time and resources, and may even impair healthy brain development by inducing excessive stress in the child.[25]

Four major aspects of infant/toddler development illuminate the kinds of "basic sensory, social, and emotional experiences" that are "essential for optimizing the architecture of low-level circuits" in the brain.[26] The following four aspects of infant/toddler development call for a special approach to planning and supporting their learning:

1. Infants follow their own learning agenda.
2. Infants learn holistically.
3. Infants experience major developmental transitions in their first three years.
4. Infants are in the process of developing their first sense of self.

The following overview describes these distinct aspects of infant/toddler learning and development.

1. Infants follow their own learning agenda

All humans are internally driven to learn and develop, but this internal drive functions in slightly different ways and degrees at different points in life. With regard to the content of

learning, the infant's learning agenda is much more focused on fundamental competencies than an older child's agenda is. The foundations for later learning in all domains are set during infancy. For example, infants and toddlers are primed to:

- seek and form relationships with people who will nurture and protect them;
- learn language for the first time in order to communicate;
- construct knowledge of basic concepts such as the relationship between cause and effect and how things move and fit in space;
- master rudimentary small-muscle and large-muscle skills.

Infants actively engage in mastering different components of these competencies at relatively similar times in their development. The common path of learning and development that infants are on, however, completely depends on ongoing interaction with adults. Without adults, infants are unable to pursue their learning agenda. In fact, part of their learning agenda is to interact with adults to have essential relationship experiences. Understanding this learning agenda helps adults interact with infants and toddlers in ways that best facilitate the children's learning and development.

The *California Infant/Toddler Learning and Development Foundations* reflect the birth-to-three learning agenda. Most babies are predisposed to seek out relationships and develop the skills that will help them survive and prosper in their early months and years. Typically developing infants are internally driven to communicate with others, to move, to explore and manipulate objects, and to solve problems. Thus, for adults to introduce their own learning agenda to infants is inappropriate. For infants, there is no strong need for adults to present specific topics for mastery or to provide the motivation to learn. Rather, infants focus on the topics of greatest importance without prompting from adults. What infants need from adults are interactions and experiences that closely match the birth-to-age-three learning agenda.

2. Infants learn holistically

Infants and toddlers take in information continuously, naturally, and fluidly. Although they often focus on one thing at a time, that focus can change quickly. From their actions, interactions, and observations, they pick up all kinds of information that they use to build knowledge and skills. A single interaction can lead to learning about many things in many areas. Although a child may start an experience by focusing on something of interest in one domain, the physical, emotional, intellectual, social, and language components of that experience are processed almost simultaneously. The infant mines each interaction for all its information.

Because infants and toddlers learn in a holistic way, they may not always focus on the content area that an adult may wish to emphasize. If adults structure interaction with the purpose of creating specific outcomes in a particular content area—for example, language or shapes—they will often miss the child's larger learning experience. Thus, plans to help with infant learning are best created in ways that reflect the child's openness to all aspects of an experience.

For example, a teacher may think that crafting a special lesson on colors will result in specific learning about color, but infants do not separate their lessons according to distinct topics. For the infant or toddler, narrowing the focus to the adult's interest or goal does not match how the child engages in learning. The child's focus may switch to the part of the interaction that is personally more important, such as the texture of the materials used to display color, the movement of the wrist to transfer the color from brush to paper, the emotional tone used in the interaction, or the social style the adult uses to introduce the activity. From the perspective of the infant or toddler, the lesson (or lessons) learned may end up having nothing to do with colors. Thus, adults can better facilitate learning by attending

to the many learning possibilities that exist for an infant or toddler in a particular experience.

3. Infants experience major developmental transitions in their first three years

During the first three years of life, much of a child's life is organized around issues related to security, exploration, and identity. While children attend to all three issues throughout infancy, each of these issues generally takes center stage at different points in development. As an issue becomes more or less prominent, developmental transitions occur. The child's behavior starts to change and reflects a new way of organizing experiences. Infant/toddler care teachers' understanding of these developmental changes helps them adapt to the children's learning processes.

Security

From birth until the age of about eight months, most infants organize their attention and behavior around developing a sense of security. In the *California Infant/Toddler Learning and Development Foundations* publication, the "Relationships with Adults" foundation describes the child at around eight months of age in the following way:

> [C]hildren seek a special relationship with one (or a few) familiar adult(s) by initiating interactions and seeking proximity, especially when distressed.[27]

During the first eight months of life, infants concentrate on seeking security, nurturance, and protection. They explore their immediate environment through the use of their senses and through their ever-expanding ability to move. With the growing awareness that they are dependent on adults for care, they begin to appreciate that they are individuals with separate identities.

Adults who provide care for young infants need to be especially attentive to the children's need to feel secure. Physical comfort, and responsive care that helps young infants regulate themselves, will build the infants' confidence in self and in the care provided by others.

Exploration

Infants' focus on security during the first eight months of life leads to organized relationship behavior. During the months that follow, infants increasingly use close relationships as secure bases for exploration. They use their growing mental and physical capacities for exploration. Captivated by the exciting world in front of them, they explore through movement, manipulation, and visual inspection. The infant/toddler "Relationships with Adults" foundation describes the infant at approximately 18 months of age in the following way: "At around 18 months

of age, children feel secure exploring the environment in the presence of important adults with whom they have developed a relationship over an extended period of time."[28]

Infants from eight to 18 months of age come to see themselves as active explorers—on their own for brief periods of time and no longer physically bound to the trusted adult. Still needing security, they check in with their secure base as they explore. They seem to be practicing independence, motivated by a powerful urge to explore, but still quite dependent on the trusted adult to be there when needed. At this age, children look to their teachers to validate their explorative bursts and to show confidence in their developing competence.

As children actively explore during this age period, adults need to adjust the ways in which they care for the infant, provide security, and relate to the child's growing sense of self. Children of this age prosper when they have a safe, secure environment and are allowed to use the teacher as a base of security from which they can journey back and forth for emotional refueling, maintaining a connection with the teacher through eye contact and vocal communication.

Identity

Children from 18 to 36 months of age change their main focus to identity. They concentrate on issues of *me* and *mine*, notions of *good* and *not so good*, and concepts of *self* and *other*. Interactions with others lead to learning about themselves as independent, dependent, and interdependent beings.

They interpret their sense of security and their explorations through this new lens. Infants now explore not only the environment around them, but also their power to change it. Frequently, they resist those who have been providing them emotional security to see how far they can go on their own and be separate. They are consumed with exploring and making choices, and they start to learn about taking responsibility for actions that result from their choices.

The foundation "Identity of Self in Relation to Others" characterizes this shift in development in the following way:

> At around 36 months of age, children identify their feelings, needs, and interests, and identify themselves and others as members of one or more groups by referring to categories.[29]

To assist children's growth toward a sense of self in relation to others, the adult needs to switch to supporting children's exploration of identity. Teachers help older toddlers with security and exploration by setting boundaries that guide children in learning rules of social behavior and by letting each child know that a trusted adult will be emotionally available during stressful moments.

These developmental transitions can be challenging for an infant/toddler teacher because the type of care has to shift as children go through rapid changes during the first three years of life. To orient curriculum planning, the foundations have been organized around the three major transitions. The teacher can be mindful of the children's major focus during each developmental period (security, exploration, or identity) while planning to support learning and development in areas such as empathy, impulse control, literacy, number sense, and large motor skills.

4. *Infants are in the process of developing their first sense of self*

One way infants build their first sense of self is through experiences of how others treat them. They receive important messages from others: "I am a person who is liked, encouraged, given choice, protected, listened to, or I am not." Infancy is when one's identity is first defined. The distinction between the infant developing a first sense of self and the older child continuing to define a sense of self first established during infancy has many implications for care. Infant/toddler care teachers influence a baby's first sense of self. They contribute to shaping the way babies see themselves.

Young babies are completely trusting and open, eagerly taking in messages from the adults who provide care for them. Babies do not judge as appropriate or inappropriate the ways in which adults treat them or what adults allow and expect them to do, but rather use adults' responses to them to build a first "opinion" of self. Although adults still have a profound influence on four-year-old children's sense of self, older children already have some sense of themselves as individuals and can assert themselves and express how they see things. For example, they may resist eating food they do not like and judge someone who tries to make them eat such food as mean or unfair. Even when infants resist eating certain foods, they do not consciously judge the person trying to feed them. Instead, they take in the ways they are treated as examples of how things are. They come to expect: "This is the way people feed me"; "This is the way people express emotions"; "These are things that cause people to get yelled at"; "These are the ways to approach people"; and "This is how my curiosity is accepted." Thus, creating a warm, caring, personal relationship with the infant is more than a nice thing to do; it significantly contributes to a child's positive sense of self.

What the distinct aspects of infant/toddler development mean for teaching and care

The four aspects of infant development call for teaching and care that is individually adapted to who infants and toddlers are and who they are becoming. Because infants move through distinct developmental periods so rapidly, adults need to respect and be responsive to each child's learning agenda. Because early learning is holistic, plans to facilitate infants' learning should reflect consideration of all the domains of development that may be influenced by an experience. Because infants relate to security, exploration, and identity formation differently at different times during development, adults can be most effective when their responses to each child fit with the child's developmental level. And finally, because infants are in the early stages of becoming aware of themselves as individuals and do not yet judge the appropriateness of messages they receive from others, adults need to be particularly sensitive to their role in shaping each infant's sense of self. An understanding of the uniqueness of infancy leads to the following question: Based on what is known about infant and toddler development, how can curriculum planning optimally meet the children's emerging knowledge, skills, abilities, interests, and needs?

Curriculum Planning

Infants and toddlers have an amazing capacity to engage in learning and organize vast amounts of new information. Clearly, an infant or toddler who is exploring how something works or interacting with an adult or other children reveals an active mind that is discovering and making sense of the surrounding world of people and things.

Infants and toddlers experience the world and build knowledge holistically during simple moments of play, exploration, and interaction with objects and with other people. They constantly

gather new information and make sense of it. Their minds actively take in sounds, words, patterns of movement, and the actions and reactions of people, creatures, and objects. They integrate new information into an increasingly complex system of knowledge. As infants expand their encounters with objects and people, they try out emerging skills, discover new actions, and experience feelings in new ways. In moments of play, they experiment, investigate, and invent solutions, trying to figure out how things work.

Just about every waking moment, infants and toddlers are busy developing fundamental competencies upon which a lifetime of learning will rest. These fundamental competencies are described in the California infant/toddler learning and development foundations. As stated earlier, during the first years of life, children begin to develop their identity, understand and regulate their emotions, and build social knowledge and skills. Concepts at the core of science, mathematics, social studies, language, literature, and the arts also have their roots in the fundamental competencies developed during infancy. For example, as infants explore how things fill up, fit in, and move in space, they build concepts that relate to physics. As infants put one block into a basket, and then another, they develop number sense. As they delight in imitating the expressions and actions of a friend while playing, they build concepts related to social science. As they share a book with a teacher, pointing to the photo of a dog and saying "Dah," followed by another "Dah," they expand their comprehension of language and interest in books, the roots of literacy. Infant care teachers can support each of these experiences through thoughtful curriculum planning. This curriculum framework guides teachers in planning curriculum that connects with children's development of emerging concepts and skills.

Planning infant and toddler curriculum requires that teachers understand and respect how infants and toddlers learn. As described previously, infants and toddlers have an inborn drive to seek information and experience. When they play, they often initiate learning, actively building skills, concepts, and connections between ideas. The development of thoughts into new concepts and actions, feelings into a sense of identity, and words and phrases into representations of thoughts, ideas, and feelings often occurs simultaneously. As infants actively engage in such holistic learning, the teacher's role is to provide possibilities for them to encounter, explore, and investigate.

Contexts for Infant/Toddler Curriculum

In planning curriculum for the birth-to-age-three period, teachers must be aware of what infants and toddlers do in play, both when they act on objects and when they interact with adults and peers. In essence, play is the "work" of infants and toddlers. When teachers are mindful of the ways in which each infant experiences a moment of play, that child's learning agenda reveals itself. In response, teachers are able to plan curriculum that aligns with the infant's inborn learning agenda.

In developing curriculum for infants and toddlers, teachers plan for three learning contexts:

1. **The play environment as curriculum.** Curriculum plans include the selection of play materials that add interest and complexity to distinct areas where infants and toddlers freely play. A thoughtful selection of materials invites infants and toddlers to explore experiences that challenge their emerging skills, concepts, and ideas.

2. **Interactions and conversations as curriculum.** Curriculum plans address ways of being with infants and toddlers during interaction, including nonverbal interaction, conversations, cooperation, conflicts, and times when infants express strong feelings such as delight, sadness, anger, or frustration.

3. **Caregiving routines as curriculum.** Curriculum plans include care routines, particularly mealtimes, diaper changes, and naptimes. Intentional teaching invites infants and toddlers to participate in care routines that deepen their relationship experiences and open up possibilities for building emerging skills and concepts.

The following section describes how infant care teachers can effectively plan curriculum for each learning context.

1. The Play Environment as Curriculum

Interest areas to support child-initiated learning through play

Curriculum for infants and toddlers includes ways in which teachers plan the indoor and outdoor physical environments to support play and learning. Intentionally designed play spaces for children are like a studio for an artist or a laboratory for a scientist. When the physical environment is planned with children's self-initiated learning in mind, they encounter places where they can freely explore what things are like and how things work. In such an environment, children investigate, invent, and experiment. To support children's self-initiated play and holistic learning, teachers create environments with a network of interest areas, each with a distinct focus and predictable inventory of materials, and each used by teachers to extend children's active search for knowledge. Interest areas are designed to offer a basic inventory of materials with which children can apply emerging skills and develop concepts while they play. Some examples of interest areas in an infant/toddler environment are:

- a cozy area for books and stories;
- a small-muscle area;
- a sensory perception area;
- an active-movement area;
- a creative expression area.

As teachers plan curriculum, they consider ways to augment or add new items to the basic inventory of materials in an area. Curriculum plans that focus on the play environment extend or add complexity to the children's play. With the same intent, teachers consider what adaptations should be made to provide greater access for children with disabilities or other special needs.

The following vignette illustrates how a group of infants around eight months of age use different interest areas in the care environment. It includes considerations for curriculum planning.

Jaylen and Amira, along with two other crawlers, are on a large sheet extended over the ground in the outdoor yard. In one corner, the teachers have placed several low, wide baskets, each holding a variety of objects. Their intent is to create an area with toys to grasp and discover. Jaylen crawls to the edge of one of the baskets and pauses. He peers inside and sees a variety of small rings—some metal, some smooth wood. There are also two round baskets, identical in all ways except color. One is blue, one is green. Jaylen reaches into the basket and grabs one of the wooden rings. He waves it up and down, watching it move, and then rolls up onto his side and mouths the smooth edge. He turns his gaze back to the basket. He rolls back onto his stomach, drops the ring, and reaches for one of the other rings in the basket—the metal canning-jar ring. He repeats a similar series of actions with this ring. He then turns his gaze to search for the first ring, and as he does so, he drops the one he has been mouthing. He crawls over to retrieve the first ring.

In the other corner of this outdoor play space, Amira, who has been crawling for several weeks, crawls in the direction of a low cushion, placed near a low, hollow cube that is just the right size for crawling through. (The teachers have prepared this interest area as an active-movement area.) Amira places one hand and then the other on the cushion and begins to pull up onto the soft surface. She inches her body forward in rhythmic bursts of movement and, little by little, makes it over the cushion and back down. She smiles, turns in a full circle, and moves up once again onto the cushion, this time from the opposite side.

This vignette shows two distinct kinds of outdoor play areas set up for infants who are about eight months of age. In one corner of the outdoor play area, teachers have prepared an array of objects, carefully selected to offer distinct yet similar physical properties and features that engage infants' emerging pincer grasp. In another corner, the teachers have created a space that provides a variety of low surfaces to challenge infants to crawl in new ways. Just as the indoor environment can be taken outdoors easily, the outdoor environment can be taken indoors easily. Both indoor and outdoor environments offer opportunities to create interest areas that extend children's play, exploration, and "meaning making" in multiple ways.

Uninterrupted time for exploration and play in the environment

To take full advantage of learning possibilities offered by interest areas, children need long blocks of uninterrupted time for self-initiated play. Teachers facilitate infants' self-initiated learning by thoughtfully creating interest areas and then following the children's lead. Infants and toddlers thrive when they have opportunities to explore and manipulate materials in ways of their own choosing, without interruption. Such moments of active infant play and exploration allow teachers to observe the children's play to discover what engages each infant's interest. In doing so, teachers also note individual children's developmental progress. Such notes are often useful when teachers complete the California Department of Education's Desired Results Developmental Profile (DRDP). The following vignette illustrates the value to both infant and teacher of uninterrupted play in thoughtfully created interest areas.

Teacher Angelica watches as nine-month-old Jacob plays with a small basket, which he has pulled from a collection of small baskets in a corner of the room. As Angelica observes Jacob's play, she is struck by how intently he is exploring this basket and how he seems to experiment with it in play. She continues to watch and then pulls out her notebook, which she keeps in her pocket. She writes the following:

Observation. *Jacob, lying on his stomach, holds a round, plastic, open-weave basket. He waves it with a stiff arm. He drops it to the ground and watches as it lands upright and wobbles on its circular bottom. Jacob watches as the wobbling basket slows and then stops. With his open palm, he taps the edge of the basket with enough force to set the basket wobbling again. He watches as it settles to a stop. Again he taps the edge, but this time much harder. The basket flips over. Jacob's eyes widen as he inspects the now upside-down basket lying perfectly still on the floor. Jacob slaps his hand onto the basket and moves it from side to side with his hand. As he does so, the basket makes a scraping sound against the floor. He smiles and laughs. He pushes the basket again and laughs as he makes the same scraping sound.*

Later in the day, Angelica retrieves the anecdotal note she wrote about

Jacob's play with the basket. She wants to read it to Jacob's father when he arrives to pick up Jacob at the end of the day. She invites Jacob's father to hear about Jacob's little experiment with physics—with how things move in space. (Note: By reflecting on her observation, Angelica has already begun to interpret it as an experiment with physics.) After Jacob and his father leave, Angelica adds the following to the written anecdote and puts it in Jacob's portfolio of observations.

Interpretation. *Angelica wrote: Jacob appears to be gathering information about what the basket is like and how it moves. He discovers that he can make it move in some predictable ways. He uses what he finds out about this basket to create a little experiment. It is as if he asks, "What happens when I push down on the edge of this basket?" Then he expresses excitement as he continues to explore. He seems to be expressing to himself: "Wow! It wobbles back and forth! Oh, that was fun to watch! Can I make it happen again? Oh, I didn't expect that!" The basket had flipped over. His facial expression and actions suggest he is asking: "What happens when I push down on the edge of the basket now?" And then his face and body movements express surprise, as if he were expressing: "Hmm. That wasn't what I expected. I thought it would wobble back and forth like it did before, but it is still. I'll try that again. Hmm. A noise . . . I like that! Let's see if I can make that again." In this little experiment, Jacob is building knowledge of cause-and-effect. He is also exploring how things move in space.*

2. Interactions and Conversations as Curriculum

Caring for infants and toddlers in small groups allows teachers to interact with children in ways that foster the children's exploration of ideas and experiences and expands their learning. Through verbal and nonverbal interaction, teachers act as guides, listeners, and "problem-posers" for infants and toddlers. Sometimes, based on ongoing observation, a teacher spontaneously initiates the interaction or the play. For example, a teacher might imitate a young infant's coo, sing a song, or do a finger play with one child or with a small group of children.

Of course, right from the start of life, infants initiate interaction with the adults who nurture them. As infants and toddlers develop, they initiate increasingly complex verbal interactions or conversations and experiences such as looking at a book with an adult, doing a finger play, or singing a song. Whether teachers or children initiate interactive play, in both instances the teacher's role is to observe children's responses in the moment and to watch and listen for their ideas, which may come through gestures, other body movements, facial expressions, sounds, or words. By observing and listening, the teacher may then responsively engage in interaction with the child or children. Sometimes the teacher may provide individual children with *scaffolds*, such as supportive language, ideas, or movements that will draw a child into exploring a more complex idea, concept, or movement. For example, an open-ended question is a scaffold that prompts children to extend or expand their ideas and facilitates new and more complex thinking or exploration. The following vignette illustrates how a teacher initiates an interest in labeling colors while being responsive to the child's self-initiated exploration.

> During a moment of play in the art area, infant teacher Joette watches as two-year-old Lucila picks up a wooden frame that encloses two sheets of blue plexi-glass. Lucila puts her eyes up close to the plexi-glass and peers through. She holds the frame out to Joette, gesturing for her to take it. Joette responds, "You want me to see what you saw, don't you? I'd love to!" Joette looks through and exclaims, "I see everything blue! Here, your turn, Lucila." Lucila looks through the block again. Another child walks up and reaches for a different frame, this one with yellow plexi-glass inside. The two children laugh together as they move the frames back and forth in front of their eyes. Teacher Joette watches and then picks up a third frame, which has red plastic sheets. She holds it near the window and a red patch appears on the floor. She gestures to the two toddlers and says, "Oh, look what's over here!" They rush to the red patch. Lucila steps onto the red patch and laughs with excitement. "It made red!" she says. "Yes!" says teacher Joette, "Will yours make a color on the floor, too? You want to try?" Lucila holds her frame to the sun, sees a blue spot, and says, "Yes, I made blue!"

3. Caregiving Routines as Curriculum

Curriculum includes ways to involve infants and toddlers in caregiving routines and to make routines an important context for learning. Daily routines provide natural opportunities for children to apply emerging knowledge and skills. Teachers integrate engaging learning opportunities into the everyday rituals of arrivals, departures, mealtimes, naptimes, diaper changes, handwashing, and setup and cleanup, both indoors and outdoors. Young

infants usually take an active interest in daily routines and respond positively when encouraged to participate. For example, when invited to choose between two outfits, a 10-month-old may look at one outfit and then the other several times before excitedly pointing at one of them. Older toddlers enthusiastically apply emerging skills during daily routines. Toddlers, for example, enjoy putting cups on the table for a meal or clearing used dishes from the meal table. As the following vignette illustrates, daily routines offer opportunities for children to build language skills, learn the rituals of sharing time with others, and relate one action in a sequence to another.

Four toddlers are seated at a low table for lunch. Their primary care teacher sits with them at the table. To his right, on a low bench, the teacher has a bin that holds everything he needs for the meal. He pulls out bibs for the toddlers and helps each toddler put one on. Each toddler finds a cube chair to sit in. The teacher puts an empty bowl in front of the toddler on his left. He offers this toddler a pair of small plastic tongs, holds a plate of small sandwiches, and asks, "Would you like to take a sandwich?" The toddler grabs the tongs and, after a few trials, manages to pick up one of the sandwiches and drop it onto his plate. Later, after each toddler has taken a sandwich, the teacher pulls from the bin a clear, plastic measuring cup, on which a red line is drawn at the one-cup mark. He fills the measuring cup to the red line. He places an empty glass in front of a toddler and, offering the toddler the measuring cup, says, "Would you like to pour?" The toddler wraps his hand around the handle and tips the cup over his glass. He spills a bit at first, but adjusts his hand and manages to empty the measuring cup. He looks up at the teacher and smiles. The teacher smiles in response, saying, "You poured your milk, Stephan! You know how to do it!" The toddler seated next to Stephan reaches for the empty measuring cup. The teacher says, "And now you can pour milk into your glass, Alexi. I'll put the milk in the measuring cup first."

Planning the Infant/Toddler Curriculum

Planning infant/toddler curriculum begins with teachers discovering, through careful listening and observation, each child's development. Observation is an essential teaching skill. When teachers mindfully observe, they find out how individual children make discoveries and make meaning within everyday moments of play and interactions. Observing for the purpose of assessing individual children's learning means carefully watching and listening with thought and reflection. In doing so, teachers find evidence of individual children's meaning-making—how a child expresses or shows feelings, how a child responds to others' feelings, and how a child responds to the impact of his actions on the objects he encounters or the people with whom he interacts. When teachers observe infants' play and interactions, they gather evidence that pertains to individual children's social–emotional, language, cognitive, and perceptual and motor development. An observation can help teachers see, describe, and understand how an infant organizes feelings, ideas, skills, and concepts. Sometimes, teachers may choose to write down what they observe in a note. They may also take a photo, or, with older toddlers, they may keep a sample of each child's work. In doing so, teachers collect observational data that provide clear, vivid evidence of children's development. Observing how children explore and play with newly introduced materials or ideas often makes it possible for teachers to track children's developmental progress on various measures of the DRDP, as the following vignette illustrates.

> *Li is an 18-month-old toddler. Each day, she brings her teacher, Carol, a favorite book about farm animals. Li's mother had told Carol how much Li loved that particular book, and Carol placed a copy in the book interest area. Carol begins to wonder how she might support Li's interest and build on it to add increasingly complex play encounters for Li and the other young toddlers in the room. She and her co-teachers discuss possible materials to add to the interest areas. They decide to take Li's favorite book, which has a photo of a farm animal on each page, make a color copy of each page, laminate the copies, and attach self-sticking fabric (e.g., Velcro) to the back of each copy. They put these photos in a basket near a felt board, which is on the back of a shelf divider in the Building and Balancing interest area. They place a play barn, with plastic farm animals, nearby. They also borrow plastic animals from other rooms in order to have a varied selection of animals, some that are similar and some that are identical in all features except size and so forth.*
>
> *They collect farm-animal puppets and put them in a basket in this interest area, and they add a selection of other cardboard books about farms or farm animals. Before the teachers finish adding materials, they discuss how these additional possibilities for play and explorations might help the children build some of the foundational competencies for this age—for example, in the areas of language development, social play, number, space and size, classification and matching, and interest in books, stories, songs, and recognition of symbols. In a review of the recently completed infant/toddler DRDPs, which provided profiles of individual children's progress in different foundational competencies, the teachers agreed that their curriculum ideas might offer a way to observe the toddlers' emerging competencies that relate to some of the infant/toddler DRDP measures for which they wished to collect additional evidence.*

As teachers observe children's play, exploration, and interactions, they discover ways to support children's learning. Ideas for the next steps in curriculum planning emerge as teachers reflect on how they might extend or expand children's exploration, problem solving, thinking, interactions, and language. Observation, reflection, and documentation in the moment simultaneously launch an ongoing assessment of each child's progress in learning as well as the curriculum planning cycle.

The Curriculum Planning Cycle

Observe, reflect

Observing and reflecting on each moment means being present with children and attentive as they interact with others and the environment. This mindful presence is different from participating in children's play or directing their play. Whether for one minute or 15, an attentive, mindful presence means watching and waiting to see what happens, moment by moment, as infants and toddlers play. By watching, wondering, and reflecting, teachers gain an increasingly complete picture of children's exploration and discovery. When observing children mindfully, a teacher will discover small scientists at work—gathering information, comparing, making assumptions, evaluating assumptions through their actions, experimenting, and, over time, building mastery of a wide range of concepts and skills.

Document, reflect

Documenting means gathering and holding evidence of children's exploration and interests for future use. A common form of documentation in early care settings is a written note, often referred to as an *observation anecdote*. Other forms of documentation include photos, video recordings, and work samples (for older toddlers). Documentation serves a dual purpose. First, it holds memories of teachers' observations of children's learning—the children's expressions of feelings, ideas, concepts, and skills. Teachers can use anecdotal notes and other evidence to deepen their understanding of children and to support periodic assessment of each child's progress (as measured by the infant/toddler DRDP). Second, documentation guides teachers as they determine next steps in ongoing, day-to-day curriculum planning to expand and make more

complex possibilities for infant and toddler learning.

Reflect, discuss, plan

As teachers reflect on infants' and toddlers' exploration and interactions, they discover possibilities to sustain, extend, and help children make their play more complex, and thereby support the children's continuing learning. Teachers review ideas for possible next steps in the curriculum. These steps might include adding materials to interest areas to offer new experiences or experiences that challenge emerging competencies; expanding infants' participation in care routines; or being intentional about engaging infants in conversations about certain topics. Teachers include in such plans ways to support the learning of individual children, always adapting the experiences to ensure full participation of children who have special developmental needs. The following vignette is an example of how one teacher and her co-teachers devise a plan.

> Sylvia, a teacher of young toddlers, decides it is time to invite her group of children to begin using serving utensils and small pitchers during meals. When she does so, she notices that the children struggle a bit but are genuinely interested in using these tools. Sylvia and her co-teachers, Sandra and Tatyana, reflect on the toddlers' strong interest but still-emerging skills in using these tools. The teachers discuss ways to add simple tools to the interest areas in order to expand opportunities for the toddlers to use them. They collect a variety of simple tongs, spoons with fairly short handles, bowls, cups, and spatulas. They place the new objects in several baskets in the Math and Physical Sciences interest area. They also plan to continue to offer toddlers a chance to serve themselves during meals and to observe how the toddlers' skills develop.

Implement, reflect

Once a plan is written, teachers implement it. While implementing a plan, teachers observe, reflect, and document. The curriculum planning cycle begins again (or continues) as teachers watch to discover how children respond to the planned curriculum and how children show evidence of their development during the planned learning encounters. Teachers often approach this step with a sense of wonder, for they may be surprised and amazed by the children's responses. To hold the responses in memory, teachers may record notes, take photos, or label, date, and keep track of older toddlers' work samples, all of which can be reviewed at a later time. In such reviews, teachers assess the impact of the curriculum plans to come up with additional ideas for supporting the children's learning. At the same time, they assess individual children's learning. For example, teachers might reflect on the following questions:

- Are children responding as we had predicted, or were there surprises?

- What do the children's responses reveal? How might the children's interests or intentions be described? What concepts and ideas are the children forming within their play?

- Are children showing evidence of progress on any of the measures of the DRDP?

The following vignette describes how Sandra, Sylvia, and Tatyana reflected on their observation and documentation of an idea they implemented.

At their next planning meeting, Sandra, Sylvia, and Tatyana gathered to share the observational notes each had written in response to adding the new utensils. Sylvia noticed Germaine moving the large spoon inside one of the tall, hollow cylinders in the Building and Balance interest area, as if he were mixing something. Sylvia decided to put this observation in Germaine's portfolio, in the section on cognition. The teachers wondered about ways to include Leah, a toddler who uses a feeding tube, in the experience. They met with Leah's parents to explore the following question: Are there ways to incorporate Leah's ways of taking meals? Working with the parents, the teachers decided to find a cloth doll and sew onto the doll's stomach a patch consisting of self-sticking fabric, so that the toddlers could attach to it a pretend feeding tube and pretend syringe. The teachers also wondered about ways to include kitchen utensils made of materials other than plastic, such as bamboo or metal, to expand the toddlers' exposure to the physical properties of these materials. They also decided to post near the sign-in area a brief photo document of the toddlers' utensil play, in order to invite the children's families to bring in safe utensils for the play—and they planned to make a special request for utensils that might be typical of each family's home culture.

The Reflective Curriculum Planning Process

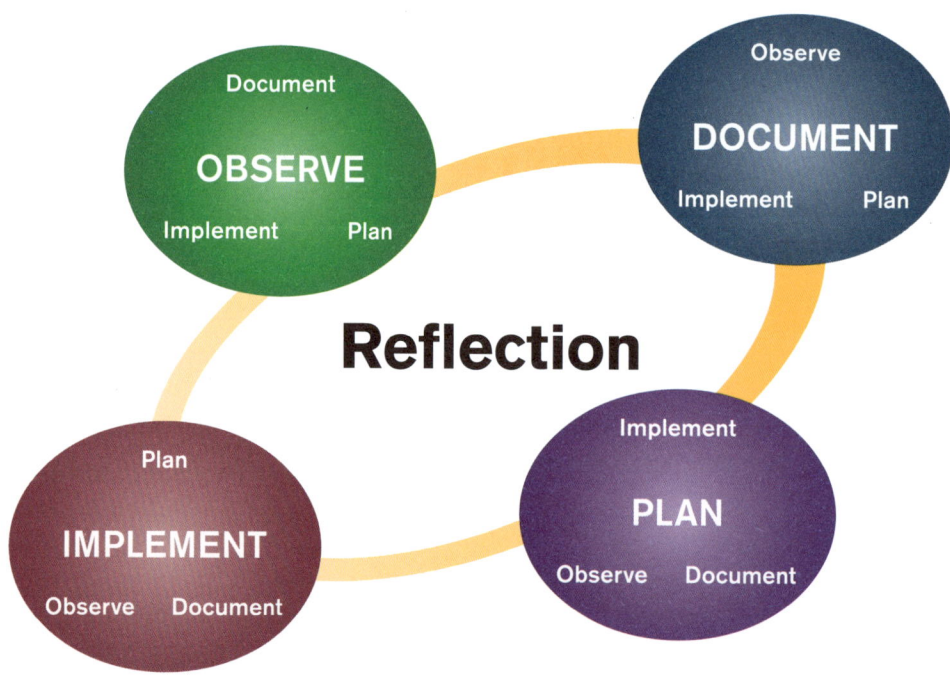

Partnering with families in planning curriculum

As several vignettes in this chapter illustrate, curriculum planning involves three partners: the infant, who actively pursues her or his own learning agenda; the infant's family members, who provide the primary relationship experiences for the infant and are the first teachers that support the child's learning and development; and the infant care teacher, who forms relationships with the infant and family, learns from them, and offers insight and guidance that brings the partnership together. Each has a unique perspective in shaping the design and the direction of the curriculum, and each relies on the other to implement the curriculum effectively. Teachers find it particularly helpful to share documentation of children's learning with the children's family members. When families and teachers reflect together on documentation of children's exploration and learning, family members offer insights into the children's behavior and ideas, as well as share expectations of their children at home or in the community. Teachers and families together discover ways to connect the children's experiences in the infant/toddler program with their experiences at home and in the community.

Infants' and toddlers' experiences at home and in their communities are a powerful source of connections for them. Teachers nurture children's appetites for learning and meaning-making by building upon the knowledge children bring to the infant/toddler setting. When teachers embed elements of the children's home and community in the infant care program, the children encounter familiar concepts, language, and materials in the program. This familiarity creates fertile ground for meaning-making and helps infants and toddlers explore with comfort and ease. Connecting the experiences at home with those in the infant center also brings coherence to the infant's or toddler's moment-by-moment experiences of meaning-making. Just as important, connections between the home and the program also support children emotionally and socially. This emotional support helps infants feel secure and allows them to explore and experiment with new objects and take on and solve problems in a new setting. The key is to get to know the families well to find out which connections are meaningful for each individual child. When teachers discover what may be personally meaningful for a child, there is a good chance of fully engaging that child in meaning-making and learning.

The following sections examine components of the curriculum planning process in greater depth. Strategies for observation, reflection, documentation, assessment, planning, and implementation are considered in more detail and in the broader context of the teaching–learning relationship. The focused look at each of these parts of curriculum planning gives insights into the teacher's role. At the same time, it is important to keep in mind that all of these parts work together simultaneously.

Reflections on Observation, Documentation, Assessment, and Planning

Observation and Documentation

Observation and documentation serve many purposes. Together they offer a way to gain a better understanding of an infant's or toddler's developmental progress, thereby informing how to support learning and providing a base for curriculum planning. From observation and documentation, teachers gain insights into ways to adapt the environment, adjust to a particular child's way of interacting, and expand on a child's interests. Observational records also serve as a valuable history of the child, which teachers and the child's family may enjoy.

When observation and documentation are part of a curriculum planning process, teachers mindfully watch infants while actively engaging with them. In so doing, teachers discover the children's interests, abilities, feelings, and needs. They can see what occupies infants' minds and bodies. Infants' gestures, looks, sounds, and actions convey what interests them and what they are trying to figure out. Teachers selectively take notes to document things that they find meaningful. This approach to observation is active and participatory. Teachers use their knowledge and all of their senses as they observe, take notes, reflect on, and interpret children's behavior. They constantly ask themselves what the children's actions mean in order to better understand each child, to plan curriculum, and to share observations with the children's families. Observation also focuses on relationships in the infant/toddler program, revealing valuable information about child–teacher, child–child, teacher–teacher, child–family member, teacher–family member, and teacher–child–group relationships.

Mindfully observing while still actively participating in a child's care may be described as participatory observation. It is different from traditional observational child study in which the observer sits quietly and unobtrusively, stays physically and psychologically separate from the children, records observations in a factual manner, and avoids making assumptions, predictions, or interpretations. In contrast, when infant care teachers observe, they actively participate in care, remaining emotionally and physically available to the children. They are responsive to children, interact with children, and still provide care while observing. As they observe, they give full attention to what is going on with the infants. This mindful presence enables teachers to gather information about the infants that is useful in understanding the children's development and in supporting their learning.

When observing, infant/toddler care teachers note both verbal and nonverbal aspects of the child's behavior as well as the context for the behavior—namely, the actions of nearby adults, other children near the child who is being observed, aspects of the environment, time of day, and so on. Sometimes teachers make a mental note when they are caring for infants or interacting with them. Later, teachers may write down what they observed earlier. Other teachers may routinely carry a notepad so that when they see something noteworthy, they can jot it down as soon as possible. In some instances, one member of an infant/toddler care teacher team will observe while the other member of the team interacts with the children. Above all, infant/toddler care teachers make sure that the need to observe for curriculum planning does not interfere with nurturing the children. In all cases, teachers should place greatest priority on being responsive to the immediate needs and interests of the children.

Mindful observation occurs throughout the day—during caregiving routines; at drop-off and pickup times; during cleanup times and transitions; and while children spontaneously engage in play, exploration, and interactions. Infant care teachers may choose to focus on particular aspects of development or exploration, such as these:

- individual attributes and temperamental traits of each child
- signs of vulnerability and competence of each child
- nonverbal and verbal interactions each child has with other children and adults
- ways in which the small group of infants functions
- each child's explorations of materials and places in the environment

As they observe, teachers pose various questions in their minds. These questions may include the following:

- What is each infant noticing, sensing, feeling, experiencing, understanding?
- What meaning is each child making?
- What ideas or hypotheses is each child exploring?
- What do the children experience as a small group primarily cared for by one or two teachers?
- How are the teachers influencing each situation?
- What might a family member like to know about the child or the group?

The type of observation that informs curriculum planning focuses on all

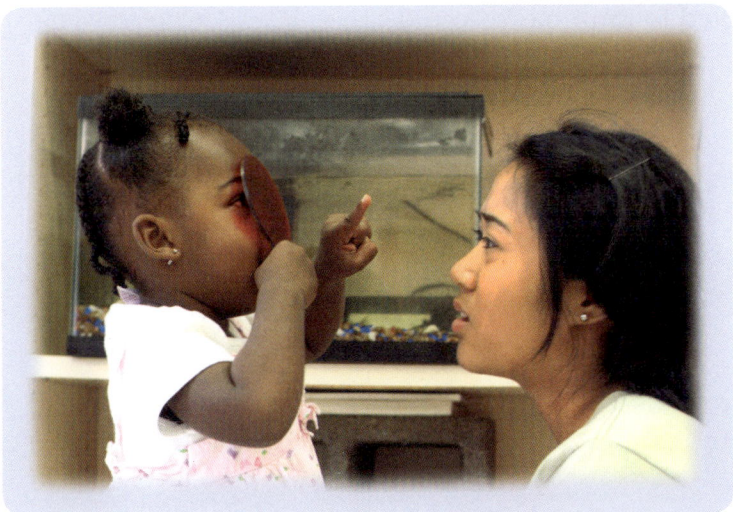

aspects of the teacher's experiences with infants and toddlers. The teacher focuses first on the child's interests but is open to everything that occurs. For instance, a teacher may see that a child watches, reaches for, and eventually approaches shiny things, such as a necklace, metal bell, or chrome water faucet. When the child picks up a shiny bell, the bell makes a noise—and the child quickly learns how to repeat the noise many times by shaking the bell. In exploring this object, the child has made a discovery about cause-and-effect relationships. The teacher then stores in memory (notes and holds in memory) observations such as this one, which will help in planning how to assist the child with exploration and making discoveries about other objects.

However, during the same observation the teacher may also notice and address barriers to learning. For example, the teacher may see that the child is unable to hear the soft ring of the bell when there are loud sounds nearby, such as the crying of a baby or tumbling block towers. Information about such barriers feeds directly into planning how to facilitate learning. In this example, the environment may need to be adapted to limit background noises.

Observation and Documentation and the PITC Responsive Process

In the Program for Infant/Toddler Care (PITC) approach to infant/toddler care, responsive teachers are always observing children. "Watch," or observation, is the first step of the PITC's three-step responsive process. Observation enables teachers to read infants' cues and meet their needs moment by moment. One of the central practices of the PITC is helping babies to establish secure bases for exploration and learning. The moment-by-moment monitoring of babies' messages and the prompt, contingent responses that stem from observation strengthen relationships between infants and their teachers and lead to the development of secure bases.

PITC's "Watch, Ask, and Adapt" process works hand in hand with curriculum planning that includes observation, documentation, and assessment. Infant/toddler care teachers observe in order to be responsive and build relationships with infants. In this process, teachers also observe and document, which helps them to deepen their understanding of children's learning and development and discover ways to support it.

The Responsive Process*

Step One:

WATCH

Begin by just watching, not rushing to do things for the baby.

Watch for both verbal and nonverbal cues.

Step Two:

ASK

Ask yourself: What message is the child sending?

What are the emotional, social, intellectual, and physical parts to the message?

Does the child want something from me at this moment?

If so, ask the child: What is it that you want?

Step Three:

ADAPT

Adapt your actions according to what you believe to be the child's desires.

Watch how the child responds to your actions.

Modify your actions according to the child's response and watch, ask, and adapt again.

*Adapted from the WestEd Program for Infant/Toddler Care *Trainer's Manual: Module I, Social–Emotional Growth and Socialization* (Sacramento: California Department of Education, 1995), pp. 41–43.

Observing While Participating

One of the key challenges for infant care teachers is to be able to observe and record their observations while providing early care and education. Learning how to address this challenge takes time and a good support system. Teachers can develop plans together for observing and recording behavior within the context of daily routines and events. Some teachers take turns; others have systems such as cameras and note cards placed around the indoor and outdoor areas so they can take quick notes or photos "on the fly." There are many ways to participate and observe at the same time. Children become accustomed to teachers who take notes and photos; the process of observing and recording behavior becomes a regular part of daily routines. Observations from teachers who are involved with children on a daily basis are the most useful because the teacher understands the child's context, everything from how the child slept the night before to his current interests. Infant care teachers who observe regularly are better able to provide care and education that connects with each child in the group.[30]

Observing and Listening

By observing and listening to children with care and attention, we can discover a way of truly seeing and getting to know them. By doing so we also become able to respect them for who they are and what they would like to communicate to us. We know that to an attentive eye and ear, infants communicate a great deal about themselves long before they can speak. Already at this stage, observing and listening is a reciprocal experience, because in observing how the children learn, we learn.

— L. Gandini and J. Goldhaber, in *Bambini: The Italian Approach to Infant/Toddler Care*[31]

Tools for Documenting Observations

Documentation tools include notepads (both paper and electronic devices), audio-recording devices, video or DVD recorders, and cameras. Teachers also include in their documentation items produced by older children such as drawings.

Each documentation method yields different information. By using multiple types of documentation tools rather than just a single tool, teachers can often gain a more complete picture of a child's learning and development.

For example, video recordings do not necessarily capture complete information, because a significant action may occur outside the focus of the camera. For this reason, it may be helpful to make notes after using a video camera to create a more complete record.

Analysis, Interpretation, and Use of Documentation

When teachers review anecdotal notes, photos, video or DVD recordings, and samples, they piece together stories that portray the development of the infants and toddlers in their care. For example:

- Teachers may gain insights by watching the same video-recorded interaction several times. This type of review may lead to editing video clips to create a sequence of key moments. The edited video material might illuminate how one learning experience connects with another. Notes about the context for a child's behavior can add new meaning to a video record.

- Teachers may put a set of photographs side by side to show a sequence of actions or learning experiences. This technique can shed light on a wide range of learning (for example, a child's understanding of routines or a child's fine motor development).

- Teachers may compare observation notes several weeks after completing an observational assessment of a child's developmental and learning progress. The observation notes may clarify why a child is making rapid progress in one developmental domain while continuing to practice at about the same level of competency in another domain.

- Teachers may review multiple pieces of documentation (video recordings, notes, photographs, and so forth) to deepen their understanding of an individual child.

There are myriad possibilities for increasing one's appreciation of early learning and development through the study and interpretation of anecdotal observations, photos, and work samples. Such documentation has the potential of serving multiple purposes. For example:

- Notes, photos, and videos may be used to make visible a learning focus of a child. For example, a teacher may document over several days a child's interest in naming objects. The documentation may include notes on new words the child has recently learned, photos of the child's pointing behavior, and notes on the types of things that particularly interest the child.

- Photos of the pretend play of older toddlers may be organized for dis-

play in the room. The children may look at the photos of their play and use ideas suggested by the photos to continue exploring pretend play.

- Teachers who team together in a room may plan based on observation and documentation. They may reflect on documentation taken over several days that shows children's cruising behavior. In studying and discussing the documentation, the teachers may decide to add a new piece of equipment in the room to provide the children with an opportunity to explore their newly developing motor skills.

- Teachers may combine photos with notes to create a book of a child's learning experiences to share with the child's family. They can look at each child's book with family members to share the child's joy of learning.

- Notes, photos, and other items collected by a teacher can be used as documentation for a DRDP measure. This documentation may provide justification for rating a child at a certain level of a measure ("Responding with Reflexes"; "Expanding Responses"; "Acting with Purpose"; "Discovering Ideas"; "Developing Ideas"; or "Connecting Ideas"). For example, a set of photos that show a child's exploration of how things fit and move in space may be used to support a rating on the "Understanding Space" measure of the DRDP and also be included in a book that is shared with the child's family.

Based on ongoing observation and reflection, documentation continually gives insights into each child. These insights deepen teachers' understanding of each child's development, which can be shared with the child's family as well as guide planning to facilitate the child's next steps in learning and discovery.

The Context for Observation and Documentation

Teachers need support, time, and equipment to collect and piece together documentation. Observation and documentation take place within a context of primary care and often during a moment of care (e.g., when diapering, feeding a young infant, or comforting an upset child). Ongoing observation, reflection, and documentation help teachers get to know each child and, when done well, make each teacher's job easier and more enjoyable. Teachers who team together often organize their work schedules to allow one or the other to spend some time collecting and reviewing documentation. With increased emphasis on learning from observational records, infant/toddler program leaders allocate time in teachers' work schedules for the purpose of documenting, reflecting as a team, assessing development, and planning for individual children's learning. Program leaders also support teachers with equipment to record observations and make infant/toddler development visible.

Observation and Documentation and the California Infant/Toddler Learning and Development Foundations

Observation and documentation are a crucial first step in curriculum planning. To be truly useful, observation and documentation must be informed by an accurate understanding of learning and development. For that reason, studying the California infant/toddler learning and development foundations supports preparation for observation, documentation, and curriculum planning. Knowledge of the foundations gives teachers insights into the fundamental competencies that infants and toddlers develop. By observing infants with the foundations in mind, teachers see and understand so much more of what is happening during this fascinating period of a child's life.

When teachers observe, and reflect on what they observe, they can use the foundations to interpret what might be the focus of the infant's exploration and learning. In this way teachers apply what they know about infant development to the infants' moment-by-moment play and interactions. Consider the following vignette, in which the infant care teacher observes an episode of toddler play.

> *Observation.* Kaysha, a toddler, holds an empty cup under a slow stream of water that flows from a hose. The hose rests on a rock pathway, where tiny plants have grown between the flat rocks. Kaysha pours the water she gathered in the cup onto the rocks and watches as it soaks into the plants and disappears. Her gaze shifts to a trickle of water that meanders down a sloped patch of dirt and darkens the dry dirt. She bends down to touch the wet dirt. She fills the cup again. This time, she pours the water over the dirt, watching the ground absorb it. She fills her cup again and pours the water onto the dirt. She repeats this three more times. Each time the water pools on the surface of the dirt, she emits a long, excited "Yeah!" but becomes quiet when the water seeps into the dirt.

The infant teacher documented his observation of Kaysha's play with a clear, descriptive anecdote. He made no assumptions about why Kaysha did what she did. For example, he did not assume that Kaysha was happy or frustrated. Nor did he analyze the learning within the play. Instead, the teacher's focus was on accurately capturing a vivid image of the play.

With this observation available as a written anecdote—a brief story of what he observed—the infant care teacher is able to return to it later to reflect on what he observed and interpret the meaning of Kaysha's play. With an accurate record that holds the memory of Kaysha's play, the teacher can easily share the anecdotal note and reflect on it with colleagues. When teachers discuss together such written documentation, they collaborate to better understand the child's progress in learning and to develop curriculum ideas that might expand her discoveries. In the case of Kaysha's discoveries with water, what emerged from such reflection and discussion was the following written interpretation of her observed play:

> *Interpretation.* It seems like Kaysha might be thinking, "So what happens when I fill this empty cup with water and then pour it over the rocks?" And then she gets really excited when she sees that the rocks change color. So she appears to want to make it happen again and repeats her actions. It is like a little experiment. But when she pours the water on the dirt, the water disappears into the dirt, and she appears to be confused by this. It is as if she is saying to herself, "Where did the water go?" But then she seems to be looking at the dirt and how it now looks different—a shade darker in color. When she pours water on the

dirt, it is as if she has moved on to a new experiment, namely, whether she can make the dirt change color, possibly the way she made the rock change color. She seems to get excited for a moment by the little pools of water she makes. But her excitement seems to fade when the pools disappear into the ground. Maybe, in repeating her actions over and over, she is trying to make the pools not go away. Her actions get more rapid. Maybe she is thinking, "I'll try pouring lots of water really fast to see if I can make the little pools stay." It appears that Kaysha is discovering how water affects objects and changes them. She is also experimenting with amounts of water and the force of water.

In this vignette, the teacher observed mindfully and reflected on what he saw and heard. He then documented his observations.

The teacher decided to write down a brief anecdote in order to hold in memory the observed play as accurately as possible. He tucked the note away, knowing that he wanted to spend more time thinking about what he had just observed and share the note with the infant's family and his teaching team.

A written anecdote allows a teacher to remember an observation in a much more reliable way than simply depending on one's memory of what occurred in the moment. Without documentation to support an observation, the memory of a moment can easily be clouded by the viewer's beliefs about what is important and what is not, which, in turn, can lead to an emphasis on some aspects of what was observed and the omission of others. Documentation that gives a complete picture of a child's engagement in play and learning opens the door to further interpretation of the teacher's observation, as the vignette about Kaysha's play suggests.

Later, in conversation with his co-teachers, the teacher read his observational anecdote. The teachers discussed the child's actions. They interpreted what occurred, trying to piece together how the child was making meaning in the moment. They also reflected on concepts from the California infant/toddler learning and development foundations to identify and describe what they interpreted to be the child's learning.

Kaysha's primary care teacher decided to put the observational anecdote in Kaysha's portfolio. He inserted it into a section where he had put earlier documentation of Kaysha's play and interactions. This observation of Kaysha's exploration of water served as useful evidence in tracking her cognitive skills. A few weeks later, the teacher completed Kaysha's DRDP, and this documentation helped him assess accurately the level at which Kaysha was working.

Written anecdotes, photos, and samples of work make it possible for teachers to keep track of each child's interests, feelings, concepts, and skills. As the above vignette illustrates, teachers can track each child's ways of learning and their progress in development through portfolios, with each child having a portfolio of anecdotes, photos, and samples. When a teacher determines that an observation provides a good description of a child's learning and development, he or she adds it to the child's portfolio to keep evidence of the child's developmental progress.

Using observation and documentation in an integrated way helps teachers to expand their understanding of each child's learning and development on a day-to-day basis. It also allows them to gather evidence for assessments that may occur at a later time.

Assessment Based on Observation and Documentation

Teachers regularly add anecdotes, photos, or samples to a child's portfolio, which provides a basis to assess each infant's or toddler's developmental progress. Teachers use such evidence to complete formal assessments according to a regular schedule, such as every four months or every six months. Periodic assessments produce profiles of every child's developmental progress in each teacher's small, primary group of children. These assessment profiles give the teacher a general orientation for supporting each infant or toddler over a period of weeks and months; they help the teacher be sensitive to the next steps in each child's development.

Observations that teachers make while interacting with infants inform the assessment process. For instance, a teacher may observe and note that when she brings out a clean diaper during a diaper change, a child stops moving and points at the diaper until the teacher says the word "diaper," and then the child smiles and makes the sound "di." This observation could be used as the teacher determines whether the child is at the "Acting with Purpose" developmental level of the DRDP's "Communication and Language" measures. As teachers gain familiarity with the DRDP, they often find that they can use their daily observations to complete it and not have to take time out of their day for special attention to the forms. Over time, teachers collect information about each child—for example, interactions they have observed, problems solved by the children, or how children participated in a care routine. Anecdotal notes are placed in each child's portfolio. These observational notes provide evidence that teachers can use when filling out a DRDP.

When completing the DRDP infant/toddler assessment instrument, teachers also use observational anecdotes, notes, and information from the family and other teachers to determine the child's level of progress in each developmental domain. For each child, the resulting developmental profile shows developmental progress in each domain and whether the child needs additional support in particular domains.

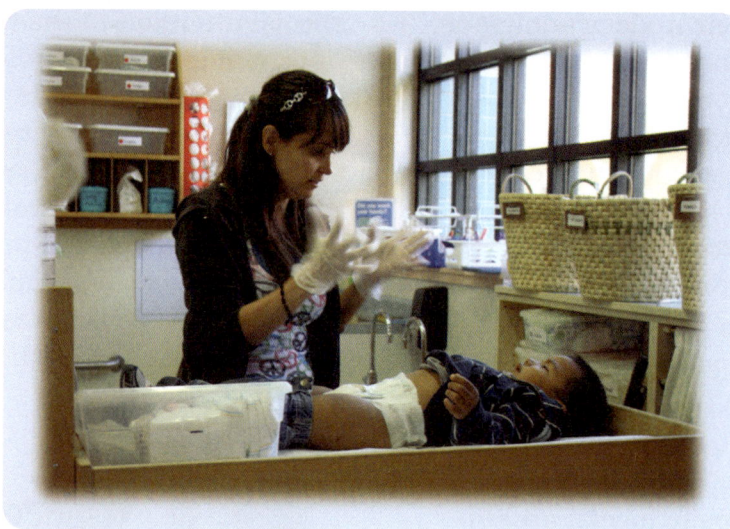

Planning Based on Observation, Documentation, and Assessment

Teachers use observation, reflection, documentation, and assessment to plan effective curriculum to support children's learning. When teachers make written records of infant/toddler play and interactions, they document children's learning. As stated earlier, to document means to intentionally record various aspects of children's experiences in the infant/toddler environment. Through documentation, teachers make visible the ways infants and toddlers learn. Anecdotal notes or photos make it possible to reflect with others on a child's (or a small group of children's) learning experiences. In doing so, teachers and parents together are able to appreciate and assess children's learning and developmental progress. Such observational evidence supports teachers in their planning of how to extend, expand, and add complexity to children's learning through effective curriculum.

> Infant care teachers study their observation records, documentation, and assessment information both individually and with colleagues and family members. Taking time to slow down, review, and think about each child's behavior, temperament, learning interests, developmental profile, and needs helps teachers deepen their understanding and appreciation of each child and gives them ideas on how to continue to support that child's learning and development.[32]

Documentation based on observation helps teachers plan for the next steps in the child's learning. It informs curriculum plans, as teachers are able to predict what each child is likely to focus on over the next days or weeks. For example, if a teacher has documented with a photo and a note that a child has begun to stand up with support, the next step for that child's motor development will be cruising—moving from place to place while standing and holding on to something for support. Knowing this, the teacher can modify the active-movement interest area to include supports on which the child might pull up to a standing position and begin to cruise around the play area from place to place. As teachers observe, reflect, and document, they become more attentive and responsive to each child's ongoing development.

In addition, teachers' reflections on observations of an individual child may lead to further reflection on the emerging interests, concepts, and skills of other children in the small group. The vignette about Kaysha's exploration of water illustrates how one child's learning focus may expand to other children.

While discussing observations of Kaysha's exploration of water, the teachers began to wonder whether other children around Kaysha's age might be interested in water and where it goes when poured on dirt or on the hard cement or rocks. The teachers brainstormed ideas on how to include experiences with pouring water in the sand/dirt area and on the cement surfaces in the yard. They noted that such experiences might be rich in opportunities to present problems to the toddlers that might engage their emerging interest in cause-and-effect and might help them experience how the different surfaces influence how the water moves. They also wondered whether they would observe how the toddlers might work together in such play. They reflected on both familiar and new vocabulary that might become a part of the children's exploration of water.

When teachers use observation and documentation to plan curriculum, they interpret children's play as a way to generate curriculum experiences that will relate to various developmental domains and that will add complexity to the learning of individual children and small groups of children. In other words, planning curriculum based on observation and documentation ensures that the curriculum will engage the children's emerging interests, concepts, and skills. Moreover, when planning curriculum with the California infant/toddler learning and development foundations in mind, teachers build on infants' interests and support their developing foundational competencies simultaneously.

Based on insights from reflection, the infant care teacher develops ideas for next steps to support each child's learning and development, including possible adaptations to interactions, environments, activities, and routines. The California infant/toddler learning and development program guidelines describe the process in the following way:

This important part of the process can be exciting and invigorating for teachers as they come up with ideas and think about how they might adapt the environment or routines or introduce a new routine or material based on observations, notes, DRDP-R information, reflection, and discussion. Part of the planning process includes reducing the list of ideas to one or two that relate directly to the interests and abilities of a child or a small group of children. Once teachers have a plan for the next step in supporting a child's learning and development, they then introduce the adaptation or change in a way that allows the child to make choices and interact freely and creatively with the new material, environmental set-up or experience.[33]

The teacher may plan to extend or support learning in particular areas, depending on the results of her review of the child's information during the reflection phase. DRDP results pertinent to the child's developmental level in different areas may inform a plan. Plans can be brief and flexible, because the general principle of responsiveness to the child's moment-to-moment interests and needs applies to this part of the curriculum planning process just as it does to other parts of the process.

A plan allows a teacher to experiment and thereby learn more about the child and about oneself as a teacher. The implementation of a plan may produce an unexpected or surprising result. A surprise, in turn, may lead to new insights: a chance to fine-tune understanding of the child through observation or communication with family members or colleagues. Thus it is recommended that programs "support teachers to implement plans in the spirit of experimentation: each time a plan works or does not work, teachers can learn and grow from the experience."[34]

Plans also present an opportunity for strengthening relationships between programs and families and for fostering family engagement in their children's care. Through the planning phase, teachers can communicate and collaborate with parents. In center programs, partnering can extend to fellow teachers and other staff members. Plans are shared to provide information about changes and to strengthen relationships with families and colleagues. Changes in routines may be a particularly important focus of communication with parents and colleagues. Communication about plans can enhance parents' feelings of inclusion in the program and provide them with opportunities to communicate about their child. Parents may also be interested in watching for changes in their child's behavior as a result of adaptations made in the child care program. Sharing plans can be a way for teachers and families to come together, enhancing their sense of partnership in the special experience of watching children grow and develop.

Implementation of a Plan

Each day, infant care teachers introduce or implement possibilities for expanding children's learning and development. Once the children in care have been observed, and their experiences documented, teachers try out their plans by making changes in the environment, introducing materials, relating to and interacting with the children in new ways, and highlighting objects or concepts for selective focus. However, this implementation process should not be seen as an end point in the curriculum planning process. Each child's unique thoughts, feelings, needs, and interests in reaction to the plan or a strategy should influence the way implementation occurs. How each infant or toddler will respond to a teacher's suggestions is unpredictable. Once a possibility or suggestion is introduced, the teacher follows along, observes what each child does, and is responsive to individual children's ongoing engagement in learning.

Like every other step in the curriculum planning process, implementation includes observation, reflection, documentation, and interpretation. Teachers note both their approach to implementation and the children's responses (or lack of response) to it. As teachers try out their plans with the children, observation and documentation have an additional focus; the ongoing study leads to further curriculum ideas to plan and implement.

Once an interaction with a child or small group of children begins, teachers have to be ready to adapt their plans and actions to the momentary and often changing needs and interests of each child. Adaptation and change are critical parts of both children's and teachers' learning processes and come into play constantly during the implementation process.

The Overall Approach to Implementation

The activities, environments, and interaction opportunities that are introduced should reflect respect for (1) the competencies that infants and toddlers bring to each interaction and (2) the children's need for relationship-based experiences. To work well, implementation should adapt to the infant's changing interests and needs during each day. In this way, the curriculum will be responsive to what the infants bring to early experiences and to what the children seek from those experiences. Implementation should:

- orient the infant care teacher to the role of facilitator of learning;
- help the teacher read the cues of each infant in the small group;
- address the whole learning experience of the children, including the learning environment and the program policies that contribute to the learning climate;
- spark each infant's interest and encourage and support exploration;
- reflect consideration for developmental stages but also allow for individual variations in temperament, approach, and pace;
- be broad enough in scope to enable the teacher to respond to all developmental domains simultaneously.

The teacher's interaction strategies are complemented by a supportive environment that offers:

- a safe and interesting place for learning;
- a variety of materials that are appropriate for the individual needs and interests of infants and toddlers in the group;
- organization of learning and care in small groups;
- adherence to policies that maximize each child's sense of security in care and continuity of relationship with the teachers;
- optimization of program connections with the child's family.

For example, a teacher may have observed over several days that a small group of older toddlers is becoming fascinated with pretend play. Among the reasons that the teacher may be attuned to this interest is its connection to several infant/toddler learning and development foundations, most notably, symbolic play. Through reflection on observations and documentation of the children's emerging interests, the teacher may decide to place additional puppets in the environment. The teacher may wonder whether the puppets would motivate the children to continue to build their interest in pretend play. Rather than drawing attention to the puppets, the teacher may simply decide to place the puppets in the dramatic play area in the room. The teacher may also add to the outside play area some new props related to gardening. Then, curious about what the children

will do with the new play materials, the teacher would wait to see what happens next. Anything could happen; the children may not be interested in the new materials, or they may begin to engage in lively pretend play that suggests new possibilities to the teacher.

The above example of supporting older toddlers' pretend play is one of countless possible ideas teachers may try out with infants as part of a reflective, responsive approach to implementation. In addition to modifying the environment and introducing equipment and play materials, teachers adapt their interaction strategies with children based on what they discover through observation, documentation, and reflection.

In another instance, a teacher may realize that the children are starting to explore the environment in a new way. With insights about the children's ongoing development, the teacher may step back when the children move out into the environment. When relating to the infants from a distance, the teacher may discover that one child may enjoy making contact from a distance, while another child may need to stay close and often seeks physical contact.

The same teacher may observe that some of the children have an emerging interest in joint attention or looking at things together with the teacher. As a result, the teacher may make a point of looking at books more frequently with children who want to look at things with an adult. When sharing books with children, the teacher may notice that two of the children spend a long time looking at each picture, while another child prefers to turn the pages quickly. Although implementing an interaction strategy to support infants' learning may start out the same way, the path each child takes with the new possibility will require the teacher to make adaptations. As soon as an interaction with an infant begins, the curriculum planning process and the PITC responsive process (Watch, Ask, Adapt) work hand in hand. For a strategy or plan based on prior observation, documentation, and reflection to be effective, the teacher has to follow each child's lead and create with the child a learning experience that is personally meaningful and responsive, moment by moment.

Tools to Support Implementation: The Program for Infant/Toddler Care (PITC) and the Infant/Toddler Learning and Development Program Guidelines Workbook

The PITC offers a great deal of information to help teachers implement curriculum plans responsively and respectfully. At the heart of the PITC is a family-oriented approach that emphasizes close relationships with infants and toddlers as the starting point for facilitating early learning and development. The PITC's responsive process enables teachers to interact with an infant spontaneously while observing the child, searching for a response that meets the child's interests or needs, and then adapting by trying out a response to the child's cues. The PITC works hand in hand with other resources in the California Early Learning and Development System, particularly the CDE publication *Infant/Toddler Learning and Development Program Guidelines: The Workbook*. This resource contains many useful suggestions for implementation, as well as activities that a teacher can incorporate individually or with a group of teachers. The workbook is available for purchase from CDE Press. For more information, visit http://www.cde.ca.gov/re/pn/rc/ or call 1-800-995-4099.

Endnotes

1. M.J. Guralnick, *Early Childhood Inclusion: Focus on Change* (Baltimore, MD: Paul H. Brookes Publishing, 2001).

2. California Department of Education, *Students by Ethnicity, State of California, 2008–09* (Sacramento, 2009).

3. Children Now, *California Report Card 2010: Setting the Agenda for Children.*

4. California Department of Education, *Number of English Learners by Language, 2008–09* (Sacramento, 2009).

5. Children Now, *California Report Card 2010: Setting the Agenda for Children.*

6. Preschool California, *Kids Can't Wait to Learn: Achieving Voluntary Preschool for All in California* (Oakland, CA, 2004).

7. California Department of Education, *Number of English Learners by Language, 2008–09* (Sacramento, 2009).

8. California Department of Education, *Preschool English Learners: Principles and Practices to Promote Language, Literacy, and Learning*, 2nd ed. (Sacramento, 2009).

9. U.S. Census Bureau, *2006 American Community Survey: United States and States—R1704. Percent of Children Under 18 Years Below Poverty Level in the Past 12 months.*

10. A. Douglas-Hall and M. Chau, *Basic Facts About Low-Income Children: Birth to Age 6* (New York: National Center for Children in Poverty, 2007).

11. Children Now, *California Report Card 2006–2007: The State of the State's Children.*

12. California Department of Education, *Special Education Enrollment by Age and Disability: Statewide Report* (Sacramento, 2008).

13. California Department of Education, *Infant/Toddler Learning and Development Program Guidelines* (Sacramento, 2006), p. 10.

14. S. Greenspan and N. T. Greenspan, *First Feelings: Milestones in the Emotional Development of Your Baby and Child* (New York: Penguin Books, 1985).

15. S. M. Bell and M. D. Salter Ainsworth, "Infant Crying and Maternal Responsiveness," *Child Development* 43, no. 4 (Dec 1972).

16. California Department of Education and WestEd, *Infant/Toddler Caregiving: A Guide to Cognitive Development and Learning*, pp. 15–16 (Sacramento, 1995).

17. California Department of Education, *Prekindergarten Learning and Development Guidelines* (Sacramento, 2000), p. 39.

18. California Department of Education, *Preschool English Learners: Principles and Practices to Promote Language, Literacy, and Learning*, 2nd ed. (Sacramento, 2009), p. 43.

19. California Department of Education, *Prekindergarten Learning and Development Guidelines* (Sacramento, 2000), p. 45.

20. J. E. Hale-Benson, *Black Children: Their Roots, Culture, and Learning Styles*, rev. ed. (Baltimore, MD: Johns Hopkins University Press, 1986).

21. B. Y. Terrell and J. E. Hale, "Serving a Multicultural Population: Different Learning Styles," *American Journal of Speech-Language Pathology* 1 (1992).

22. A. S. Epstein, *The Intentional Teacher: Choosing the Best Strategies for Young Children's Learning* (Washington, DC: NAEYC, 2007), p. 1.

23. Center for Applied Special Technology (CAST), *Universal Design for Learning* (2007).

24. National Research Council and Institute of Medicine, *From Neurons to Neighborhoods: The Science of Early Childhood Development* (Washington, DC: National Academies Press, 2000).

25. National Scientific Council on the Developing Child, *The Timing and Quality of Early Experiences Combine to Shape Brain Architecture: Working Paper No. 5* (2008), p. 4.

26. Ibid.

27. California Department of Education, *California Infant/Toddler Learning and Development Foundations* (Sacramento, 2009), p. 16.

28. Ibid.

29. Ibid, p. 21.

30. California Department of Education, *Infant/Toddler Learning and Development Program Guidelines* (Sacramento, 2006), p. 101.

31. L. Gandini and J. Goldhaber, "Two Reflections About Documentation: Documentation as a Tool for Promoting the Construction of Respectful Learning" (New York: Teachers College Press, 2001), p. 126.

32. California Department of Education, *Infant/Toddler Learning and Development Program Guidelines* (Sacramento, 2006), p. 39.

33. Ibid, pp. 39–40.

34. Ibid, p. 107.

Bibliography

Bell, Sylvia M., and Mary D. Salter Ainsworth. "Infant Crying and Maternal Responsiveness." *Child Development* 43, no. 4 (Dec 1972): 1171–90.

California Department of Education. *California Infant/Toddler Learning and Development Foundations.* Sacramento: California Department of Education, 2009.

———. *Infant/Toddler Learning and Development Program Guidelines.* Sacramento: California Department of Education, 2006.

———. *Inclusion Works! Creating Child Care Programs That Promote Belonging for Children with Special Needs.* Sacramento: California Department of Education, 2009.

———. *Number of English Learners by Language, 2008–09.* Sacramento: California Department of Education, 2009. http://dq.cde.ca.gov/dataquest/LEPbyLang1.asp?cChoice=LepbyLang1&cYear=2008-09&cLevel=State&cTopic=LC&myTimeFrame=S&submit1=Submit (accessed October 18, 2010).

———. *Prekindergarten Learning and Development Guidelines.* Sacramento: California Department of Education, 2000.

———. *Preschool English Learners: Principles and Practices to Promote Language, Literacy, and Learning.* 2nd ed. Sacramento: California Department of Education, 2009.

———. *Special Education Enrollment by Age and Disability: Statewide Report.* Sacramento: California Department of Education, 2008. http://dq.cde.ca.gov/dataquest/SpecEd/SpecEd1.asp?cChoice=SpecEd1&cYear=2008-09&cLevel=State&cTopic=SpecEd&myTimeFrame=S&submit1=Submit&ReptCycle=December (accessed October 26, 2010).

———. *Students by Ethnicity, State of California, 2008–09.* Sacramento: California Department of Education, 2009. http://www.ed-data.k12.ca.us/profile.asp?tab=1&level=04&ReportNumber=16&fyr=0809 (accessed October 18, 2010).

———. *A World Full of Language: Supporting Preschool English Learners.* DVD. Sacramento: California Department of Education, 2007.

California Department of Education and WestEd. *Infant/Toddler Caregiving: A Guide to Cognitive Development and Learning.* Sacramento: California Department of Education, 1995.

Center for Applied Special Technology (CAST). *Universal Design for Learning.* 2007. http://www.cast.org/udl (accessed October 26, 2010).

Children Now. *California Report Card 2006–2007: The State of the State's Children.* 2007. http://www.childrennow.org/uploads/documents/reportcard_2007.pdf (accessed October 26, 2010).

———. *California Report Card 2010: Setting the Agenda for Children.* 2010. http://www.childrennow.org/uploads/documents/reportcard_2010.pdf (accessed October 18, 2010).

Douglas-Hall, A., and M. Chau. *Basic Facts About Low-Income Children: Birth to Age 6.* New York: National Center for Children in Poverty, 2007.

Epstein, A. S. *The Intentional Teacher: Choosing the Best Strategies for Young Children's Learning.* Washington, DC: National Association for the Education of Young Children (NAEYC), 2007.

Gandini, L., and J. Goldhaber. "Two Reflections About Documentation: Documentation as a Tool for Promoting the Construction of Respectful Learning," in *Bambini: The Italian Approach to Infant/Toddler Care.* Edited by L. Gandini and C. Pope Edwards. New York: Teachers College Press, 2001.

Greenspan, S., and N. T. Greenspan. *First Feelings: Milestones in the Emotional Development of Your Baby and Child.* New York: Penguin Books, 1985.

Guralnick, M.J. *Early Childhood Inclusion: Focus on Change.* Baltimore, MD: Paul H. Brookes Publishing Company, 2001.

Hale-Benson, J. E. *Black Children: Their Roots, Culture, and Learning Styles.* Rev. ed. Baltimore, MD: Johns Hopkins University Press, 1986.

National Center for Children in Poverty (NCCP). *California Early Childhood Profile.* 2009. http://www.nccp.org/profiles/pdf/profile_early_childhood_CA.pdf (accessed October 18, 2010).

National Research Council and Institute of Medicine. *From Neurons to Neighborhoods: The Science of Early Childhood Development.* Committee on Integrating the Science of Early Childhood Development. Edited by J. P. Shonkoff and D. A. Phillips. Board on Children, Youth, and Families National Research Council and Institute of Medicine. Washington, DC: National Academies Press, 2000.

National Scientific Council on the Developing Child. *The Timing and Quality of Early Experiences Combine to Shape Brain Architecture: Working Paper No. 5,* 2008. http://developingchild.harvard.edu/index.php/resources/reports_and_working_papers/working_papers/wp5/ (accessed October 27, 2010).

Preschool California. *Kids Can't Wait to Learn: Achieving Voluntary Preschool for All in California.* Oakland, CA: Preschool California, 2004.

Terrell, Brenda Y., and Janice E. Hale, "Serving a Multicultural Population: Different Learning Styles." *American Journal of Speech-Language Pathology* 1 (1992): 5–8.

U.S. Census Bureau. *2006 American Community Survey: United States and States—R1704. Percent of Children Under 18 Years Below Poverty Level in the Past 12 months.* 2006. http://factfinder2.census.gov/faces/tableservices/jsf/pages/productview.xhtml?pid=ACS_06_EST_R1704.US01PRF&prodType=table (accessed January 25, 2012).

WestEd, Program for Infant/Toddler Care. *Trainer's Manual, Module 1: Social–Emotional Growth and Socialization.* Sacramento: California Department of Education, 1995.

Chapter 2

The California Early Learning and Development System

Chapter 1 highlights how infants and toddlers actively engage in learning through interaction with others and through exploration of their environment. Research on high-quality infant/toddler care confirms the essential role that sensitive, responsive infant/toddler care teachers play in early learning and development. Teachers need to be knowledgeable about how infants and toddlers learn and be skillful at nurturing infants' self-initiated engagement in learning. This curriculum framework is a component of the California Early Learning and Development System, which is designed to foster the development of early care and education professionals. Each component has a specific focus. Together, the components provide a comprehensive system of support for early childhood professionals and infant/toddler programs in their work with children and families. The system includes the following infant/toddler components:

- Learning and development foundations
- Learning and development program guidelines
- Desired Results Developmental Profile (DRDP)—part of the Desired Results assessment system
- Program for Infant/Toddler Care (PITC) training system
- Curriculum framework

The infant/toddler curriculum framework highlights other components of the Early Learning and Development System and includes recommendations on how to use them. For example, chapter 1 refers to the infant/toddler learning and development foundations, and the strategies presented in chapters 3 through 6 are organized around the foundations. Guidance is given on how to use the content of the foundations, which identify three major transition points during the infancy period—at around eight months, at around 18 months, and at around 36 months. Similarly, chapter 1 includes excerpts from the infant/toddler learning and development program guidelines and

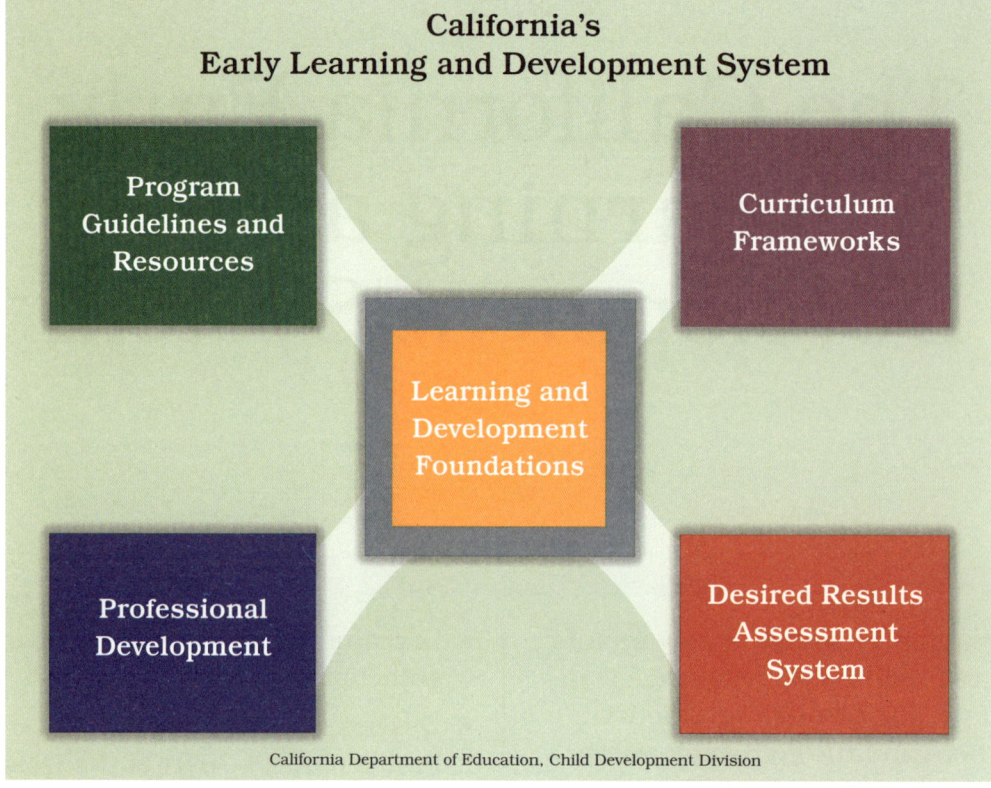

California Department of Education, Child Development Division

highlights the DRDP. The curriculum planning process described in this framework will help early childhood educators use the other four components of the system, which, in turn, are designed to enrich the use of the curriculum framework.

To support infant/toddler care teachers, the California Early Learning and Development System was built with state-of-the-art information on early learning and development and features best practices in early care and education. Each component area of the system provides resources that focus on a different aspect of supporting infant/toddler care teachers and is linked to the resources provided in every other component of the system. This chapter provides an overview of the component areas and some of the resources. One resource, the Desired Results Developmental Profile (DRDP), is described in greater detail than the others. The DRDP allows teachers to assess children's progress in key areas of learning, which is integral to curriculum planning. A description of each component area follows.

Infant/Toddler Learning and Development Foundations

California's infant/toddler learning and development foundations are central to the state's Early Learning and Development System. The foundations describe competencies—knowledge and skills—that all young children typically learn with appropriate support. They also present infant/toddler learning and development as an integrated process that includes social–emotional development, language development, cognitive development, and perceptual and motor development. The foundations give a comprehensive view of what infants and toddlers learn through child-initiated exploration and discovery, teacher-facilitated experiences, and planned environments, offering rich background information for teachers to consider as they plan for children.

The foundations identify key areas of learning and development. While moving in the direction identified by each foundation, every child will progress along a unique path that reflects his or her individuality and cultural and linguistic experiences. The foundations help teachers understand children's learning and can give focus to intentional teaching. Other resources that support intentional teaching are organized around the foundations. As explained in chapter 1 of this framework, strategies for fostering children's learning in each area are organized by the domains specified in the foundations. In addition, the DRDP is aligned with the foundations, and that alignment fosters an integrated image of each child. Unlike a developmental profile with a large number of indicators, the fully aligned DRDP provides a profile of individual children's progress in each domain. With developmental profile information focused on the domain areas, teachers will be able to use the curriculum framework to support each child's learning in various domains in an integrated way.

To support professional development focused on the foundations, the California Department of Education (CDE) developed the *California Infant/Toddler Learning and Development Foundations DVD Series*. Filmed at diverse infant/toddler programs around the state, the DVD clips bring the foundations to life, illustrating the behavior described in the foundations through the behavior of a variety of children. This three-DVD set includes an introduction to the foundations, commentary on the foundations, and domain introductions as well as extended scenes (with optional commentary) that show the integrated nature of early learning.

The foundations are central to the other components of the Early Learning and Development System— namely, program guidelines, other resources, and professional development. The program guidelines and other resources cover a broad range of policies and practices that influence program quality, such as the design of indoor and outdoor learning environments, partnerships with families, cultural diversity, inclusion of children with special needs, and professional ethics. In implementing recommended policies and practices, program directors and teachers set the stage for intentional curriculum planning that aligns with the infant/toddler learning and development foundations. With regard to professional development, the CDE has initiated a multifaceted strategy of training and technical assistance that is aligned with the infant/toddler learning foundations to support the use of all resources in the early learning system.

Infant/Toddler Curriculum Framework

Ongoing classroom planning is an integral part of intentional teaching. The infant/toddler curriculum framework is the resource in the early learning system that focuses on planning for children's learning. The framework includes principles, concepts, and practices that reflect a developmentally appropriate approach to planning learning environments, interactions, experiences, and daily routines for young children. Designed to foster respect for the diversity of infants and toddlers, families, teachers, communities, and programs in California, the framework is flexible; it does not prescribe activities that teachers are expected to follow. Rather, it encourages teachers to adapt to individual, cultural, and linguistic diversity as they support children's ongoing engagement in exploration and discovery.

As mentioned previously, chapters 3 through 6 of the curriculum framework are closely aligned with the infant/toddler learning and development foundations. Each of these chapters focuses on a specific domain presented in the foundations: social–emotional development (chapter 3); language development (chapter 4); cognitive development (chapter 5); and perceptual and motor development (chapter 6). The framework is meant to support young children's learning in all of these domains. It offers an in-depth look at ways to help infants and toddlers acquire knowledge and skills in specific areas, always within the context of an integrated approach to supporting learning.

Desired Results Assessment System—*Desired Results Developmental Profile (DRDP)*

Teachers gain general knowledge of young children's learning from the foundations, and ideas for supporting learning from the curriculum framework, but neither of those resources informs teachers about individual children's learning and developmental progress. The Desired Results Developmental Profile (DRDP) infant/toddler instrument, a component of the CDE's Desired Results system, is the resource in the early learning system that assists teachers with documenting individual children's progress. The DRDP is an observational assessment instrument that is aligned with the foundations. It provides teachers with a developmental profile of each child's progress. In addition, teachers can look at the individual profiles for an entire classroom to see the extent to which all children in a group are making progress and benefiting from the teachers' classroom planning.

Information gained from the DRDP helps teachers plan for individual children and for small groups of children. As described in chapter 1, teachers review individual children's developmental profiles for any emerging knowledge and skills that might be supported. In one example, the teacher noted that a child was making progress toward pulling up to a standing position with support and toward cruising. The information from the child's DRDP led the teacher to check the environment to make sure it provided furnishings that would facilitate that kind of movement.

It is important for teachers to document individual children's learning. By doing so, they can deepen their understanding of how to support each child's learning and development. As teachers observe and document what engages children in learning, especially during child-initiated play, they simultaneously reflect on what they observe, document significant aspects by taking notes or photos, and begin to appreciate each child's creation of meaning. Ongoing observation, reflection, and documentation occur throughout each day. Teachers continually gain insights and find new ways to connect with the children's developing competencies, expand children's thinking, and encourage further exploration of an emerging idea or ability. The day-to-day documentation of children's learning experiences becomes the source for periodic assessment of children's developmental progress.

Teachers use documentation gathered over time to complete a DRDP for each child. These assessment instruments produce developmental profiles for each child across the major domains of learning and development, such as social–emotional development, language development and emerging literacy, cognitive development, and perceptual and motor development.

The resulting developmental profile for each child shows the domains in which the child has made progress and whether there are any domains in which he or she needs additional support. As discussed in chapter 1, teachers use information from the DRDP to provide each child with an appropriate level of challenge in specific knowledge and skill areas as children engage in an integrated learning experience.

To facilitate curriculum planning, the DRDP infant/toddler instrument summarizes children's progress in each learning area along a continuum of either five or six levels: **Responding with Reflexes, Expanding Responses, Acting with Purpose, Discovering Ideas, Developing Ideas, and Connecting Ideas.** Each level on this continuum is qualitatively different from the other levels. Brief descriptions of infant and toddler behavior at each level follow:

Responding with Reflexes. Children at this level produce basic responses, such as the Moro Reflex, turning the head, looking in their immediate visual field, and cooing.

Expanding Responses. Over time, as infants interact with people who care for them and explore objects in their immediate physical environment, and gain some rudimentary motor control, they move to the next level on the continuum. They add to their basic responses; for example, they start to make new sounds, gain control over head movements, reach for objects, and smile in response to pleasurable experiences.

Acting with Purpose. Children at this level begin to organize responses to accomplish goals, solve problems, strengthen their sense of emotional security, communicate, explore the environment, coordinate simple actions with others' actions, and attend to the routine actions of others.

Discovering Ideas. Children at this level explore and express simple concepts about self, others, and things; maintain attention for increasingly extended periods of time; begin to engage in cooperative interaction, such as playing a simple game; and follow guidance from others.

Developing Ideas. Children at this level anticipate situations by preparing self and taking action ahead of time; use increasingly complex language to describe self, others, routines, and events; engage in simple play around a common idea; initiate and follow through with actions; respond to increasingly complex requests; rely on past guidance; and engage in interac-

tions to share thoughts, feelings, and experiences to solve problems and make plans.

Connecting Ideas. Children at this level combine words, phrases, or actions to express themselves, play, and solve problems; follow increasingly complex sequences of actions, such as the meaning of simple stories; and communicate about future events.

At all times, young children's learning is integrated. Every experience offers them an opportunity to develop a wide range of knowledge and skills. Likewise, every experience typically involves more than a single competency as children learn. One of the most important competencies that infants and toddlers develop is language. As described in chapter 1, children who are dual-language learners use both languages as they learn in all domains. Because dual-language learners may use their home language to show understanding of specific discoveries (e.g., cause-and-effect relationships or how things fit and move in space), teachers often document and assess the extent to which a child demonstrates knowledge and skills in his or her home language. The DRDP user guide and training information provide guidance to teachers on how to document and assess competencies dual-language learners demonstrate using their home language.*

Families play an essential role in their children's learning. They know their children better than anyone else and are able to provide insights and ideas that add to teachers' understanding of children. Reflecting with family members on documentation and an infant's or toddler's individual profile of developmental progress strengthens the curriculum planning process. Partnering with families in this process honors their role in their children's learning and communicates respect. Together, teachers and families can generate ideas and activities to foster children's development of knowledge and skills at school and home.

The DRDP is part of the Desired Results assessment system, which, in turn, is part of the larger California Early Learning and Development System. In addition to the DRDP, the Desired Results system includes the Desired Results Parent Survey and the Environment Rating Scale (ERS). Information collected with the Desired Results assessment tools allows early childhood educators to review, evaluate, and reflect on:

- the strengths of their program (for example, a program may already provide a rich collection of age-appropriate books);

---

*The DRDP user guide is available at http://www.wested.org/desiredresults/training/index.htm.

- ways to increase the quality of their program (for example, a program may discover a need to partner with the children's families to increase the variety of activities and interactions it offers in support of children's perceptual and motor development, both in the infant/toddler care setting and at home);
- the effectiveness of their program's curriculum (for example, information on the children's current progress in engaging in emotion regulation would help teachers focus their curriculum planning on the area of social–emotional development).

Descriptions of the Desired Results Parent Survey and the ERS follow.

Desired Results Parent Survey

The Desired Results Parent Survey is used (1) to assess parent satisfaction with the early childhood program, and (2) to gain an understanding of families' strengths and needs in supporting their children's learning and development and in achieving their goals. Programs conduct this survey annually as part of their self-review.

Teachers reflect on responses to the parent survey to understand other information they have gathered about the children and the program, to identify program strengths, and to determine ways to facilitate family participation in the program and help family members build their capacity for supporting their children's learning and development.

Environment Rating Scale (ERS)

The ERS assesses the quality of the learning environment.* Specifically, teachers use the ERS to assess the quality of the interactions, the space, the schedule, and the materials they provide to their group of children. The ERS is completed, summarized, analyzed, and then considered in program improvement plans once a year. Teachers combine information gained from the ERS with other sources to engage in long-term planning and continuous program improvement.

Program Guidelines and Other Resources

Infant/Toddler Learning and Development Program Guidelines

The infant/toddler learning and development program guidelines recommend policies and practices that enhance the quality of infant/toddler programs. In addition to giving an overview of infants' and toddlers' learning and development and curriculum planning, the guidelines cover a broad range of topics that contribute to program quality, particularly the following:

- Providing family-oriented programs
- Providing relationship-based care
- Ensuring health and safety
- Creating and maintaining environments for infants and toddlers
- Engaging in program development and commitment to continuous improvement
- Helping teachers continue to grow professionally
- Understanding that learning and development are integrated across domains
- Implementing an infant/toddler curriculum process

---
*See Harms, Clifford, and Cryer 2005, p. 92.

As stated earlier in this chapter, the recommendations in the infant/toddler learning and development program guidelines set the stage for intentional teaching and curriculum planning centered on the infant/toddler learning and development foundations.

The program guidelines are complemented by two resources that are intended to help educators and trainers in their professional development work with infant/toddler care teachers. A workbook—officially titled *Infant/Toddler Learning and Development Program Guidelines: The Workbook*—consists of active learning experiences for each section of the program guidelines. The learning experiences promote understanding of the guidelines and advise how to implement recommended policies and practices. The workbook supports the development of a learning community in which current infant/toddler care teachers, and individuals who are preparing to become infant/toddler care teachers, have multiple opportunities to explore recommended program policies and practices and learn from one another. The *Infant/Toddler Learning and Development Program Guidelines DVD Series* presents a subset of the learning activities from the program guidelines workbook. In the DVD clips, practitioners who have completed a workbook activity discuss their experience and reflect on what they learned from it. Thus the workbook and DVDs are designed to complement each other; the workbook activities allow teachers to explore ideas firsthand, while the DVDs augment the active learning experiences by showing teachers in discussions about the insights and understanding they gained from the activities.

Professional Development

Professional development makes the California Early Learning and Development System come alive for teachers and program directors. The CDE has adopted a multifaceted approach to promoting the use of the early learning system in professional development. Initiatives include the preparation and ongoing professional development of infant/toddler teachers in two- and four-year colleges. In addition, a network has been created to support the continuing development of current infant/toddler care teachers. To guide and foster professional development, the CDE partnered with First 5 California to develop Early Childhood Educator (ECE) Competencies that are aligned with the infant/toddler learning foundations and all other resources in the early learning system.[†] These competencies describe the knowledge, skills, and dispositions of early childhood educators and will become the CDE's cornerstone for professional development, training, and technical assistance.

In-Depth Understanding and Planning for Children's Integrated Learning

The different resources and activities that make up the California Early Learning and Development System offer infant/toddler program directors and teachers opportunities for in-depth exploration of a wide variety of topics. As part of the system, this curriculum framework invites teach-

---

[†]Visit the CDE's Child Development Web site (http://www.cde.ca.gov/sp/cd/) to access the ECE Competencies and other California Early Learning and Development System resources.

ers to explore the details of curriculum planning in each domain. At the same time, rather than being isolated from learning in other domains, the strategies presented for one domain are connected with learning in other domains. By deepening their understanding of each domain, teachers can see new possibilities for integrating curriculum planning and connecting children's learning experiences. The chapters that follow explore in detail the domains of social–emotional development, language development, cognitive development, and perceptual and motor development. As the vignettes in chapter 1 illustrate, teachers draw on their comprehensive understanding of children's learning in different domains. As teachers observe, reflect on, and document each child's engagement in exploration and discovery, their knowledge of strategies that support learning in various domains helps them use an integrated approach when planning curriculum. With in-depth knowledge of how to support knowledge and skill development in every domain, teachers can more easily focus on a specific area of learning while being responsive to each child's whole learning experience.

Bibliography

California Department of Education. *California Infant/Toddler Learning and Development Foundations.* Sacramento: California Department of Education, 2009.

———. *California Infant/Toddler Learning and Development Foundations, DVD Series.* DVD. Sacramento: California Department of Education, 2009.

———. *Infant/Toddler Learning and Development Program Guidelines.* Sacramento: California Department of Education, 2006.

———. *Infant/Toddler Learning and Development Program Guidelines, DVD Series.* DVD. Sacramento: California Department of Education, 2009.

———. *Infant/Toddler Learning and Development Program Guidelines: The Workbook.* Sacramento: California Department of Education, 2009.

Harms, T., R. M. Clifford, and D. Cryer. *Early Childhood Environment Rating Scale.* Rev. ed. New York: Teachers College Press, 2005.

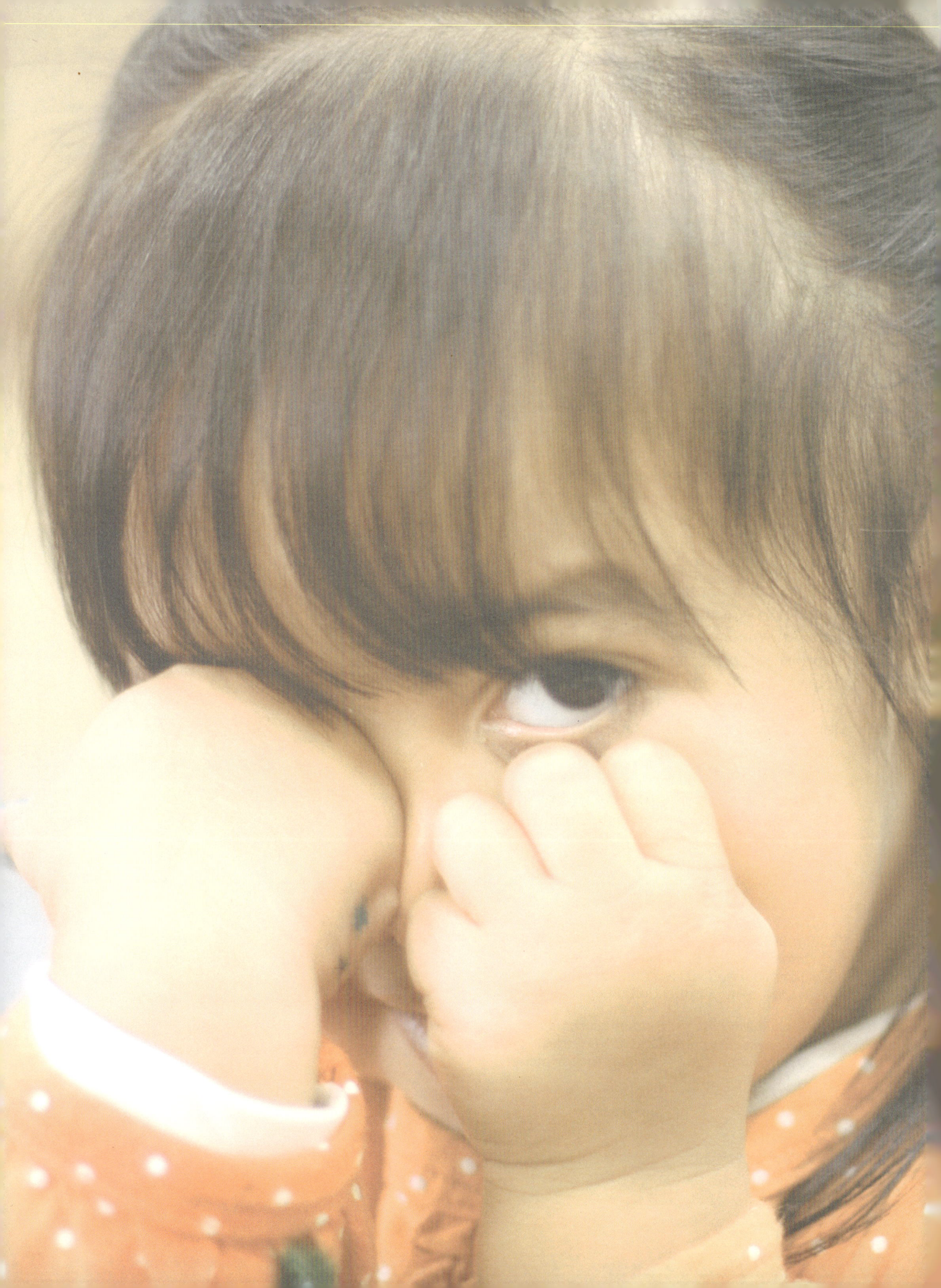

Chapter 3

Social–Emotional Development

Social–emotional development includes the child's experience, expression, and management of emotions and the ability to establish positive and rewarding relationships with others.[1] It encompasses both intra- and interpersonal processes.

> The core features of emotional development include the ability to identify and understand one's own feelings, to accurately read and comprehend emotional states in others, to manage strong emotions and their expression in a constructive manner, to regulate one's own behavior, to develop empathy for others, and to establish and maintain relationships.[2]

Infants experience, express, and perceive emotions before they fully understand them. In learning to recognize, label, manage, and communicate their emotions and to perceive and attempt to understand the emotions of others, children build skills that connect them with family, peers, teachers, and the community. These growing capacities help young children to become competent in negotiating increasingly complex social interactions, to participate effectively in relationships and group activities, and to reap the benefits of social support, which is critical to healthy human development and functioning.

Healthy social–emotional development for infants and toddlers unfolds in an interpersonal context, namely that of positive ongoing relationships with familiar, nurturing adults. Young children are particularly attuned to social and emotional stimulation, and newborns appear to be more attentive to stimuli that resemble faces.[3] They also prefer their mothers' voices to the voices of other women.[4] Through nurturance, adults support the infants' earliest experiences of emotion regulation.[5, 6]

Responsive caregiving helps infants begin to regulate their emotions and to develop a sense of predictability, safety, and security in their social environments. In the early years of a child's life, relationships are so important that experts have concluded, "nurturing, stable and consistent relationships are the key to healthy growth, development and learning."[7] In other words, high-quality relationships increase the likelihood of positive outcomes for young children.[8] Experiences with family members and teachers provide an opportunity for young children to learn about social relationships and emotions through exploration and predictable interactions. Professionals working in child care settings can support the social–emotional development of infants and toddlers in various ways—for example, by interacting directly with young children, communicating with families, arranging the physical space in the care environment, and planning and implementing curriculum.

Brain research indicates that emotion and cognition are profoundly interrelated processes. Specifically, "recent cognitive neuroscience findings suggest that the neural mechanisms underlying emotion regulation may be the same as those underlying cognitive processes."[9] Emotion and cognition work together, jointly informing the child's impressions of situations and influencing behavior. Most learning in the early years occurs in the context of emotional supports.[10] And, in the words of J. Panksepp, "[t]he rich interpenetrations of emotions and cognitions establish the major psychic scripts for each child's life."[11] Furthermore, cognitive processes, such as decision making, are affected by emotion.[12] Brain structures involved in the neural circuitry of cognition influence emotion, and vice versa.[13] Emotions and social behaviors affect the young child's ability to persist in goal-oriented activity, to seek help when it is needed, and to participate in and benefit from relationships.

Young children who exhibit healthy social, emotional, and behavioral adjustment are more likely to have good academic performance in elementary school.[14, 15] The sharp distinction between cognition and emotion that has historically been made may be more of an artifact of scholarship than it is representative of the way these processes occur in the brain.[16] This recent research strengthens the view that early childhood programs support later positive learning outcomes in all domains by focusing on the promotion of healthy social–emotional development.[17, 18, 19] In light of current research, social–emotional experience needs to be at the center of infant/toddler curriculum planning.

Guiding Principles

Learn from the family about the child's social–emotional development

Infants' social–emotional development begins at home. They begin to learn how adults respond to cues, such as crying, smiling, and cooing. Their first experiences with reciprocal interactions, language and communication, and care routines are with

family members. Through these early relationship experiences, infants start to form expectations about how people treat them, and family members gain deep understanding of their child. In light of the family's experiences with their infant, teachers have much to learn about the child from the family. Through partnerships with families, teachers can gain important information on how to support infants' social–emotional development and find ways to build on the children's learning and development at home.

Place relationships at the center of curriculum planning

The most fundamental need of infants and toddlers is to have close, nurturing relationships that help them build a sense of emotional security. Chapter 1 of this curriculum framework states, "Relationships provide infants and toddlers a secure emotional base from which they can explore and learn. Much of the cognitive, language, social, and physical learning a child experiences occurs while interacting with an adult." Because relationships are at the core of infant/toddler learning and development, teachers start curriculum planning by considering how to facilitate positive relationship experiences. Teachers look for ways in which the learning environment can be arranged to facilitate their interactions with children and the interactions that children have with each other. Teachers provide enough play materials so that children are more likely to engage in positive play rather than struggle for control of an insufficient number of materials. As teachers observe children in play, they watch for opportunities to be responsive to a child's needs, recognize a child's accomplishments, show interest in a child's exploration and discovery, make suggestions that help children solve problems, engage in back-and-forth interaction, and provide a secure base for children's exploration and learning.

Read and respond to children's emotional cues

As stated in chapter 1, emotions drive early learning. Infants and toddlers are active, curious learners who experience pleasure when receiving a positive response from a nurturing adult or when making a discovery. The pleasure children experience motivates them to continue engaging in positive interactions, exploring, and learning. The emotional responses of infants and toddlers express their interests and needs. It is important for teachers to read the children's cues to pick up on learning interests and meet needs. By reading emotional cues, teachers determine whether to engage in interaction with a child or to wait quietly to see what the child will do next. Emotional cues let teachers know if children are ready for more interaction, want more complexity added to their play, or are tired and need quiet time. Responsiveness to a child's emotional cues strengthens the teacher–child relationship and opens up new possibilities for the child's learning in the social–emotional domain and in all other developmental domains.

Attend to the environment's impact on children's social–emotional development

The child care environment affects the social–emotional development of

infants and toddlers in various ways. If the environment is set up to make it easy for children and teachers to make eye contact and communicate with each other, teachers can be emotionally and physically available to children, and the children can develop a secure base for learning. Children need comfortable places where they can be close to a teacher to look at a book, do a finger play, or have a quiet conversation. Care routines are more emotionally satisfying in environments that are arranged for interaction and the children's participation. Additionally, group size is an important factor that influences the impact of the environment; a learning environment with a small number of children will keep the amount of stimulation at a manageable level for both the children and the teachers. The environment also influences everyone's mood—children and teachers alike—and the amount of stress experienced in the child care setting. An environment with ample fresh air, peaceful colors, different kinds of lighting, places to move freely, and easy access to play materials promotes a sense of calm that allows children and teachers to focus on exploring and learning together.

Understand and respect individuality

Each infant or toddler is unique. Temperament, family experiences, culture, language, and other biological and environmental factors blend together to influence each child's development. Another consideration is whether a child has a physical disability, sensory impairment, or other special needs. Uniqueness may be reflected in a child's approaches to learning, rate of development, and ways of relating to others. The following statement from the California Department of Education publication *Infant/Toddler Learning and Development Program Guidelines* summarizes how teachers can support a child's social–emotional development in particular and his or her learning and development in general:

> Each child will approach and explore his or her environment and relationships differently. Some children need specialized support from an attentive adult to help them actively explore

their worlds and build relationships with other people. Other children naturally seek out these experiences through self-discovery and activity. Although most children generally follow a fairly similar developmental path, some children have differences in their development due to their disability, experiences, or inborn traits. Understanding each child's development is part of the joy and responsibility of the teacher. If the child's development varies from the expected path, the teacher needs to monitor it, communicate with the family, and determine how best to support the child.[20]

To be emotionally responsive to each child, a teacher needs to form close, respectful relationships with the child and the child's family. The teacher can learn about the uniqueness of each child through these relationships and can discover how to help each child adapt to the infant/toddler care setting and continue to develop socially and emotionally.

Summary of the Foundations

The social–emotional development domain consists of 11 foundations:

1. Interactions with Adults
2. Relationships with Adults
3. Interactions with Peers
4. Relationships with Peers
5. Identity of Self in Relation to Others
6. Recognition of Ability
7. Expression of Emotion
8. Empathy
9. Emotion Regulation
10. Impulse Control
11. Social Understanding

Please refer to the map of the social–emotional development foundations on page 78 for a visual explanation of the terminology used in the infant/toddler learning and development foundations.

Environments and Materials

Environments that support the social–emotional development of infants and toddlers have small groups, primary and consistent caregivers, individualized scheduling, appropriate teacher-to-child ratios, and culturally responsive, family-oriented care. Such environments allow children to (1) learn about themselves and others, (2) develop a sense of self-confidence and self-efficacy, (3) understand their feelings and the feelings of others, (4) positively express their feelings and respond to the feelings of others, and (5) learn to develop positive relationship and conflict-resolution skills. To support social–emotional development, teachers use the following strategies.

Create a positive environment that allows children to explore freely, in which they often hear "yes" and seldom hear "no."

Provide materials that support relationships and the development of social understanding. Include pictures of families, teachers, and children in the environment, displayed in the children's play area on small cards or homemade books. Self-adhesive fabric can be used to attach pictures to walls. Additionally, place pictures of family members on a peek board

pet stores, buses, trains, restaurants, and offices.

Provide materials that relate to feelings and emotional expression. Offer books, stories, songs, and pictures about feelings. Display throughout the classroom photos of different feelings—possibly around a mirror, where children can see their own faces and photos of various feelings. Use puppets, dolls, and stuffed animals to tell stories about feelings, with a focus on simple themes: sad to say good-bye, afraid of the dog, mad or sad when another child takes a toy away, or frustrated because climbing on tables is not allowed. With materials such as these, a simple story can be told that demonstrates a feeling, the cause of the feeling, appropriate ways to express the feeling, and a resolution.

Arrange the environment to support peer interactions and relationships. Create environments where small groups of children can explore materials and each other freely. Nonmobile babies placed on their backs, 1 to 3 feet apart, are able to see and hear each other. Toys that are soft and easy to hold provide opportunities for children to give and take toys

(two pieces of poster board fastened together, with pictures glued to the bottom piece and doors cut in the top piece for children to open) or on several sides of a milk-carton block (made by cutting a milk carton in half, pushing one into the other, and covering with paper, pictures, and clear adhesive paper). Include in the environment artifacts from families that children can look at, listen to, or play with—for example, cloth, hats, vases, candles, music, and clothes. Add puppets and flannel-board figures for children to use in dramatic play. Set up dramatic play areas where children can practice relationships and roles; examples of pretend settings include homes, bedrooms, kitchens,

with other children. Create individual, small-group, and open spaces in the environment. It is helpful to offer places where children can feel "alone" (e.g., individual cardboard boxes, carpeted riser boxes, cubby spaces); small spaces where a child can be with one or two friends; and open spaces where groups of children can gather together. Include pictures of the children into the care environment; post pictures of all the children in the group, low on the wall so children can see them. Make a collection of small cards, each with a picture of a child in the group. Laminate the cards or cover them with clear contact paper. Make a small book (with loose-leaf rings or ribbon) that displays pictures of children in the group. Provide multiples of popular toys so children can engage in parallel and associative play; doing so also reduces peer conflict.

Interactions

Interactions with adults are fundamental for infant/toddler social–emotional development. Caregiving routines that occur throughout the day offer particularly important learning experiences for infants and toddlers because they happen regularly and consistently. By experiencing and participating in these routines, children learn what it means to be nurtured in a caring way. In supportive relationships with adults, children also learn what it means to engage in reciprocal, responsive interactions. Over time, they begin to learn to do things for themselves. They develop competence by predicting how the routine will go, knowing how their bodies work, learning how to read their body signals, and learning how to participate in their care. Primary caregiving allows infants and toddlers to learn another person's communication and interaction style. Through primary caregiving, a young child learns to predict what will happen in interactions with her teacher. She and her teacher learn one another's ways of communicating.

As stated throughout this publication, observation and responsiveness are essential curriculum tools. They are particularly important in supporting social–emotional development. Observation enables an infant care teacher to try to understand a baby's behavior and to respond promptly and appropriately. These responses let the baby know that she is an effective communicator and initiator of events. Observation also makes it possible for an infant care teacher to create interesting and meaningful interactions with children. For example, when a teacher observes young toddlers pouring water from a tub onto the ground and looking at her expectantly, she can comment with words such as *pouring*, *splashing*, *wet*, *empty*, or *full* and can plan for future water setups that use different containers, to find out where the children's interests might lead.

To support social–emotional development, teachers:

Offer learning opportunities through caregiving routines. Develop predictable caregiving routines (diapering, napping, feeding, dressing, washing, arrivals, and departures) that foster a sense of security in a baby. Let children know ahead of time what is going to happen and develop a predictable sequence for the routine. Include the child in the routine. Tell him what you are going to do and describe your actions. Encourage him to participate in every way he can.

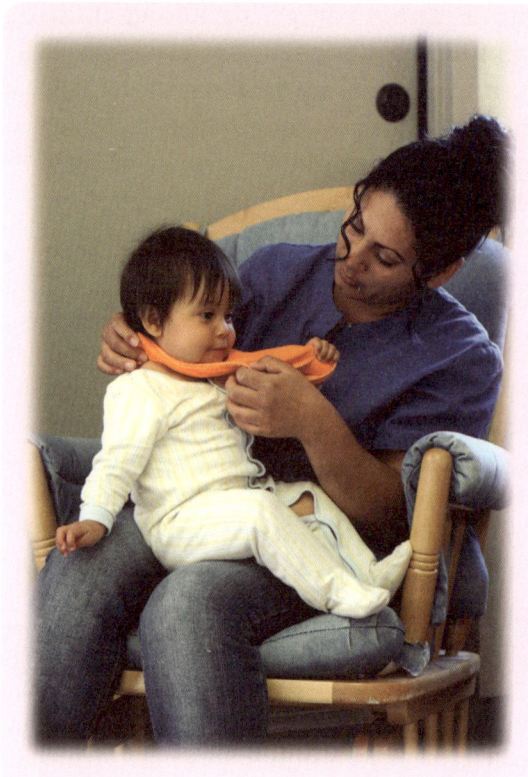

Additionally, share the lead with a child during caregiving routines. A teacher may want to carry out the routine, but often the child has another agenda. While including the child in the routine, a teacher listens and responds to the child's behavior, emotional expressions, and vocalizations or speech. Allow an infant or toddler to participate in feeding—for example, by having the child watch a spoon and open her mouth for the food, choose her bib, reach for and hold her spoon, self-feed, drink from a cup, pour her drink, serve herself, or help with cooking activities. Implement "warming-in," in which children and families who are about to begin child care visit a few times with the teacher in the program setting, and the teacher visits the child and family at their home.

Learn about temperament. This applies to the temperaments of the children in the program and to your own temperament. Adapt to each child's temperament. For instance, provide ample outdoor time for an active, high-energy child, and provide extended warming-in time for a "slow-to-warm" child. Notice when children have temperaments that are personally challenging, and work to adapt caregiving to meet each child's needs.

Pay attention to feelings and emotional responses. Help children name their feelings. Instead of telling children what they feel, suggest to them names for feelings. This strategy gives children a vocabulary about feelings and also communicates that they are the ones who know what their feelings are.

In addition, help children to understand what causes their feelings. Offer children—rather than tell them—possible explanations. Pay attention to your emotional responses, as young children are keenly sensitive to tone of voice and facial expressions. Furthermore, model for children respectful, appropriate expressions of emotion, facial expressions, and tone of voice that match their feelings. Loud or intensely angry tones can be overwhelming and frightening for children.

Support and respect the child's relationship with his or her family. Build respectful, caring relationships with each child's family members. Use your communication with families as a model of interpersonal communication for the children to observe. Discuss with family members how routines are done at home. Think about ways to include each family's caregiving practices in the care you provide. Talk to children about their families. Use a child's home language when possible. Use rhymes or songs from the child's family. Show children pictures of their family members. Remind children that their family members are thinking about them, love them, and will be back to pick them up. Talk about family memories with children.

Support relationships and interactions among the children in the program. Acknowledge children's healthy impulses, model appropriate behavior, use positive direction and choice, give information, and ensure safety when children are interacting with each other. Appreciate the ideas children try to test or express. Model the behavior that you want children to learn. Give positive directions, such as "Be gentle with your friend." Redirect children and offer choices. Offer information about consequences of children's actions.

Provide continuity of care to support children's relationships with teachers as well as children's relationships with one another.

Model responsive and respectful interactions and behavior. Be sensitive to turn-taking in interactions with babies. After approaching or communicating with a baby, wait a few moments to give her a chance to respond. Tell the infant or toddler in advance what you are going to do. For example, let an infant know, with verbal and nonverbal cues, that you are going to pick him up. This type of communication helps a young child learn what to expect from relationships. Additionally, acknowledge the presence of new adults who come into the environment and provide information about them.

Respect children's interests. If you want to do something with a child who is already engaged with a person or activity, wait and observe briefly to find an appropriate moment to get the child's attention. Listen and respond to children's vocalizations and speech, even when you are unable to fully understand them.

Support children's regulation of emotions. Learn each child's preferred ways to be comforted. Identify or name for children what helps them feel comforted. Acknowledge when children seek comfort and comfort themselves. Collaborate with children in providing comfort for them. Keep in mind that children are capable of helping to comfort themselves.

Demonstrate acceptance for all of the feelings children express. Young children use social referencing, which means they look to adults throughout the day to "read" how things are going. When someone is crying, a teacher can provide a calm, accepting, and empathic tone to help children learn that crying is natural and related to feelings of sadness, frustration, fear, and anger. Likewise, a teacher who responds calmly when angry or afraid helps children learn that such feelings are valid and appropriate.

Vignette

Anita is holding six-month-old Jed on her lap. Jed is the first child to arrive in Anita's family child care home each day. They have a few quiet minutes together before the other children begin to arrive. Anita has noticed that Jed often demonstrates excitement when watching the older children. He kicks his legs and puffs his breath when he sees Carlo and his mother enter the playroom. Miss Anita turns so that Jed can easily see Carlo and she says softly to Jed, "Here is Carlo, coming to play. He made you laugh yesterday, didn't he?" Anita smiles and greets Carlo and his mother, and then she says, "Carlo, Jed is so happy to see you. Do you see how he kicks his legs and waves his arms? Would you like to say hello?" When Carlo approaches, Anita says to Jed, "Here is Carlo, coming to say hello." The boys gaze at each other quietly for a moment. Anita is attentive and silent. Then Carlo makes a silly face and dances, and Jed lets out a little giggle. Carlo's mother, who is several months pregnant, shares a smile with Anita.

Responsive Moment

Anita recognizes Jed's interest in Carlo and knows that the two had a pleasurable encounter the day before. Anita responds to Jed's interest by positioning him so he can see Carlo and by encouraging Carlo to greet Jed. Anita wants Jed to have a chance to pursue his interest, and at the same time help Carlo learn to recognize that even tiny babies are people with feelings, interests, and skills. Anita skillfully guides Carlo's attention to Jed's interest and animated movements. Carlo and Jed share an important moment in which they learn about each other and have a chance to see and be seen. Through moments such as this one, Anita gently and intentionally supports the young infants in interacting with older children throughout the day.

Vignette

At the infant/toddler center, two children, Kristen and Edgar, are sitting together by the door. Both children are about 30 months old. Their primary care teacher, Celia, has told them that if they go get their shoes from the shoe shelf, she will take them on a walk in the nearby woods. Edgar has been at the center only for a week, but his almost immediate connection with Kristen has helped him to settle in quickly. They chatter excitedly to each other about their walk in the woods. It will be Edgar's first time there. Kristen tells Edgar how she will chase the squirrels on the path, as she did on her last walk. Kristen, whose right hand has a tiny thumb and no fingers, sits down to put on her shoes. Edgar notices Kristen's hand and, with concern in his voice, asks, "Where your fingers? Is it hurt?" Edgar reaches out to touch Kristen's hand as if this is the first time he has noticed, though he has asked about it a few other times. Kristen quickly tucks her hand under her arm. Teacher Celia sits down with the children and offers to help with the shoes as needed. She holds out her hands and says to both children, "Kristen has one big hand and one small hand." Kristen holds both hands in front of her and looks at them. Edgar holds out his too, and the two children look at their hands together. Kristen grabs one shoe, puts her foot in it, and uses her small thumb as a wedge to get her heel into the shoe. Edgar, with a serious expression on his face, places his shoes in Celia's lap, and she puts them on for him. Kristen reaches out and tugs on his shoe, and he laughs because this action made him feel ticklish. Then the teacher and two children walk out the door, holding hands and looking for squirrels.

Responsive Moment

Celia wants to support the developing friendship between Kristen and Edgar and also help them work through the potentially difficult moment when Edgar asks about Kristen's hand. Kristen will likely be asked about her hand repeatedly throughout her life. In fact, at 30 months of age it is likely that she has already been asked about her hand several times. So Celia knows that this moment provides Kristen with an opportunity to learn how to handle this kind of question effectively. The situation also provides Edgar with a chance to see that Kristen's condition is a part of her, but not all of her. In discussions with Kristen's parents, Celia has asked how they would like her to handle questions about Kristen's hand. The parents and Celia have agreed that Celia could simply describe Kristen's hand to other children, without getting into complicated explanations about the cause or effects of Kristen's condition. In this particular situation, Kristen has already mastered how to put on her shoes and is able to help Edgar, who has not yet learned this skill. In other situations, Kristen may need some extra help from others.

> ### Research Highlight 1
> How do infants and toddlers come to understand the thoughts and feelings of people around them? Infants and toddlers pay close attention to what others are doing and feeling. Toward the end of the first year of life, infants begin to follow another's gaze or gesture (joint attention), and they use the emotional cues of others to provide them with information about an unfamiliar situation to help guide their actions (social referencing).[21] Recent research suggests that in addition to using direct emotional cues, 18-month-olds engage in "emotional eavesdropping"—the use of indirect emotional information to regulate their actions.[22] Older infants pay attention not only to emotional information directed toward them, but also to emotional information directed toward others in their environment, using both kinds of information to guide their actions.

> ### Research Highlight 2
> Emotion regulation is recognized as a key component of children's social and emotional competence and is considered foundational to children's later social and academic success. Research indicates that caregivers play a central role in helping infants regulate emotions, and that early on in development infants rely almost exclusively on caregivers to help them regulate their emotions.[23] Caregivers who respond to infants' negative and positive emotions in sensitive and contingent ways promote infants' abilities to regulate their own emotions. Notably, infants who tend to get frustrated and upset more easily are likely to receive even greater benefit from caregivers who read their cues and make efforts to help them manage their distress.[24]

Sample Developmental Sequences

Identity of Self in Relation to Others

Definition: Children' social–emotional development includes an emerging awareness that one's sense of self is both distinct from and connected to others.

Beginning level: Children begin to communicate their needs to caregivers. For instance, they may move their arms and legs when seeking attention or turn their head toward an adult during caregiving routines.

Next level: Children use their senses to explore themselves and others. For instance, they may examine their own hands or feet by looking at them or mouthing them, or they may touch an adult's hair when it is within reach.

Next level: Children can recognize their own selves, familiar people, and familiar things. They show clear awareness of being a separate person and of being connected to other people. For instance, they respond to someone who calls their name or turn toward a familiar person upon hearing their name.

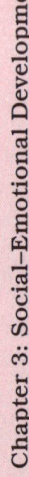

Next level: Children not only recognize but also can communicate their own names and the names of familiar people and things. For instance, a child may point at a picture of herself and say her name, or point to a peer and say that person's name.

Next level: Children become more aware of their own preferences and characteristics and those of others. They may express more details about themselves and their connection to other people and things by referring to categories. For instance, they may use family roles, such as "Brother," "Baby sister," "Mommy," or "Daddy."

Recognition of Ability

Definition: As children mature, they are gradually able to evaluate their own abilities to do things and show interest in others' evaluation of self. They develop the sense that they can make things happen and that they have particular abilities.

Beginning level: Children communicate their needs until those needs are met. For instance, they may cry when hungry until they are fed.

Next level: Children show pleasure while repeating simple actions. For instance, they may smile while kicking.

Next level: Children experiment with different ways of making things happen, persist in trying to do things even if faced with difficulty, and show a sense of satisfaction with what they can do. For instance, they may try to roll or creep to another part of a room even when there is a barrier.

Next level: Children show interest in others' reactions when exploring their own abilities. For instance, they may finish painting a picture and hold it up to show a family member, or they may insist on zipping up a jacket when an adult tries to help.

Next level: Children seek an adult's attention ahead of time in order to demonstrate abilities. They try to get the adult to watch by calling, motioning, or pulling before they do something. For instance, a boy may say, "Watch me! Watch me!" and then demonstrate that he can put on his coat by himself.

Engaging Families

Engaging families in supporting the social–emotional development of their infants and toddlers starts with the relationship between early care and education programs and families. Infant care teachers and families can model positive relationships for children through open communication and mutual respect. Additionally, suggestions offered in daily conversations,

meetings between teachers and family members, or newsletters can engage families in understanding and facilitating their children's social–emotional learning and development at home and in the program setting. Such communication also helps family members appreciate that emotional development works hand in hand with intellectual and language development. Teachers should make efforts to:

- Develop rituals for certain routines, such as separations and reunions, which meet physical needs, provide comfort during stressful times, and convey a sense of predictability, consistency, and stability.

- Respond to children's cues through actions, words, and facial expressions.

- Minimize infants' exposure to excessive stress and protect children from both overstimulation and understimulation. As developmentally appropriate, provide language to help children learn to recognize and regulate a range of emotions (e.g., "I see that you're starting to get excited" or "It sounds like you're frustrated").

- Make sure that expectations for emotion regulation, impulse control, and attention are developmentally and individually appropriate—for example, by limiting the time that children spend waiting and by keeping promises made to children ("I'll get you some milk after I put these books away").

- Model empathic behaviors and help family members build their child's social understanding by communicating with their child about the thoughts and feelings of others. For example, a teacher may wonder out loud why another child is crying or suggest ways to help the child feel better.

- Strengthen the children's sense of self and connection to others; bridge their social worlds by asking family members to share stories, traditions, or objects from home in the infant/toddler care setting. Also, encourage family members to mention their child's peers and infant care teachers during conversations at home.

Questions for Reflection

1. How can you communicate with families about the relationship between social–emotional development and learning and development in other domains?

2. What are some ways that you can learn about family and cultural influences on social–emotional development (including the expression of emotion, expectations for emotion regulation, and so forth) for the children in your group or program?

3. How can daily and personal care routines provide a sense of predictability, security, and nurturance for children? How can you make them more socially and emotionally meaningful for children? How can you include families in planning how you carry out routines?

4. In the curriculum planning process, what strategies have you implemented that were specifically intended to facilitate children's social–emotional development? What engaged the children and helped them learn? What

else might you do in the future to facilitate children's social–emotional development?

Concluding Thoughts

Developmentally appropriate curriculum planning for infants and toddlers begins with each child's social–emotional development. The child's relationship experiences are at the core of social–emotional development. Infant/toddler care teachers can best foster the child's learning by understanding every important relationship in the child's life. Likewise, a partnership with the child's family provides a window on the child's emotional life. Insights from the family, combined with the teacher's observations of the child, help the teacher understand the uniqueness of each child and find ways to be responsive to each child's preferences, abilities, temperament, interests, and needs. The teacher's responsiveness strengthens the developing relationship with the child and establishes a secure base for the child's exploration and learning. The child's emerging capacity for self-regulation, which includes emotion regulation, impulse control, and attention maintenance, is bolstered by gentle, respectful guidance from nurturing adults. With an emotionally secure base and with guidance that supports self-regulation, infants and toddlers can concentrate on exploration and learning in every domain.

Map of the Foundations

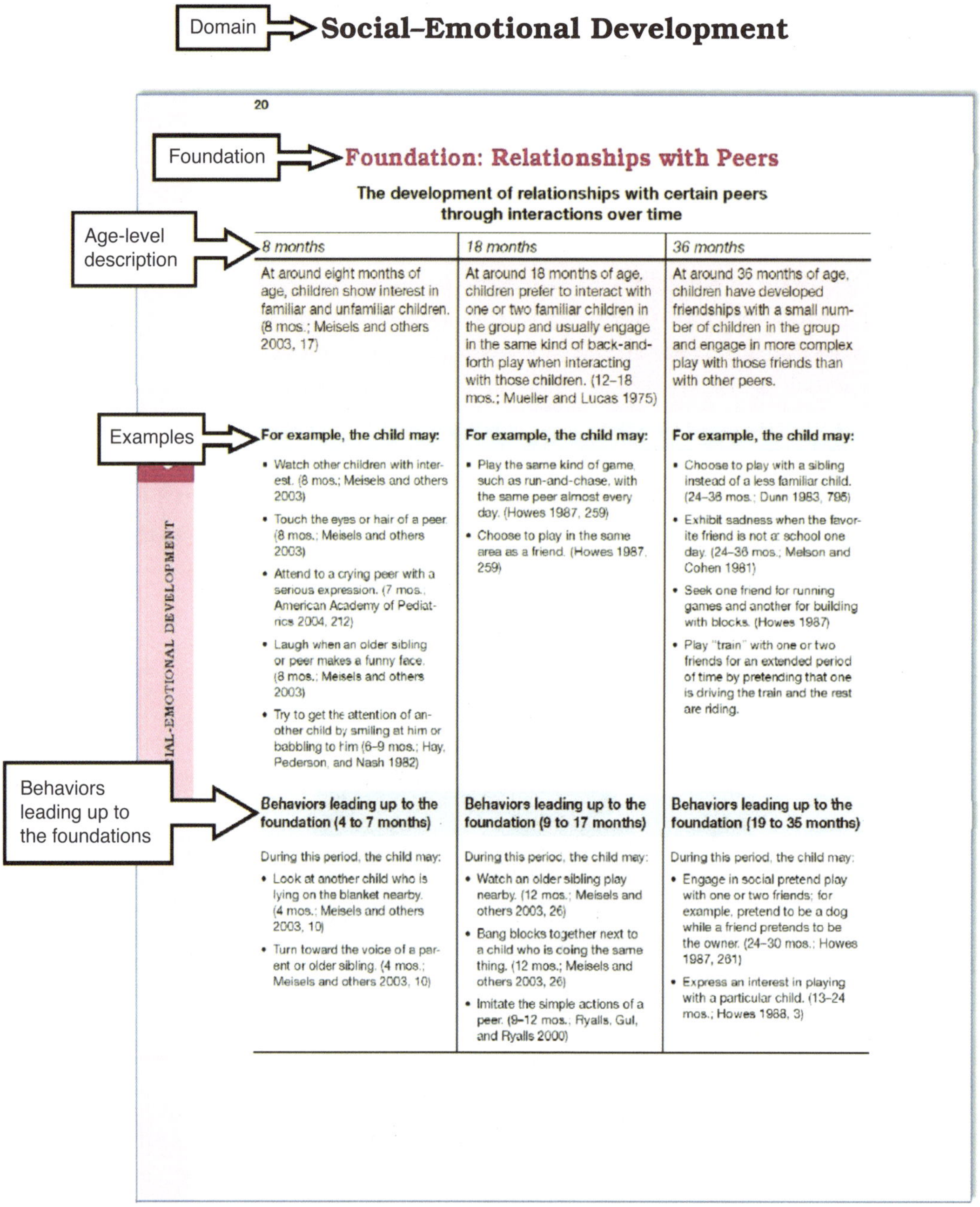

Domain → **Social–Emotional Development**

20

Foundation → **Foundation: Relationships with Peers**

The development of relationships with certain peers through interactions over time

Age-level description →	8 months	18 months	36 months
	At around eight months of age, children show interest in familiar and unfamiliar children. (8 mos.; Meisels and others 2003, 17)	At around 18 months of age, children prefer to interact with one or two familiar children in the group and usually engage in the same kind of back-and-forth play when interacting with those children. (12–18 mos.; Mueller and Lucas 1975)	At around 36 months of age, children have developed friendships with a small number of children in the group and engage in more complex play with those friends than with other peers.
Examples → **For example, the child may:**	• Watch other children with interest. (8 mos.; Meisels and others 2003) • Touch the eyes or hair of a peer. (8 mos.; Meisels and others 2003) • Attend to a crying peer with a serious expression. (7 mos.; American Academy of Pediatrics 2004, 212) • Laugh when an older sibling or peer makes a funny face. (8 mos.; Meisels and others 2003) • Try to get the attention of another child by smiling at him or babbling to him (6–9 mos.; Hay, Pederson, and Nash 1982)	**For example, the child may:** • Play the same kind of game, such as run-and-chase, with the same peer almost every day. (Howes 1987, 259) • Choose to play in the same area as a friend. (Howes 1987, 259)	**For example, the child may:** • Choose to play with a sibling instead of a less familiar child. (24–36 mos.; Dunn 1983, 795) • Exhibit sadness when the favorite friend is not at school one day. (24–36 mos.; Melson and Cohen 1981) • Seek one friend for running games and another for building with blocks. (Howes 1987) • Play "train" with one or two friends for an extended period of time by pretending that one is driving the train and the rest are riding.
Behaviors leading up to the foundations →	**Behaviors leading up to the foundation (4 to 7 months)** During this period, the child may: • Look at another child who is lying on the blanket nearby. (4 mos.; Meisels and others 2003, 10) • Turn toward the voice of a parent or older sibling. (4 mos.; Meisels and others 2003, 10)	**Behaviors leading up to the foundation (9 to 17 months)** During this period, the child may: • Watch an older sibling play nearby. (12 mos.; Meisels and others 2003, 26) • Bang blocks together next to a child who is doing the same thing. (12 mos.; Meisels and others 2003, 26) • Imitate the simple actions of a peer. (9–12 mos.; Ryalls, Gui, and Ryalls 2000)	**Behaviors leading up to the foundation (19 to 35 months)** During this period, the child may: • Engage in social pretend play with one or two friends; for example, pretend to be a dog while a friend pretends to be the owner. (24–30 mos.; Howes 1987, 261) • Express an interest in playing with a particular child. (13–24 mos.; Howes 1988, 3)

Teacher Resources

Brault, L., and T. Brault. *Children with Challenging Behavior: Strategies for Reflective Thinking.* Phoenix, AZ: CPG Publishing Company, 2005. http://www.braultbehavior.org/ (accessed November 30, 2010).

Brazelton, T. B. *Touchpoints: The Essential Reference: Your Child's Emotional and Behavioral Development.* Reading, MA: Addison-Wesley, 1996.

Bredekamp, S. *Effective Practices in Early Childhood Education: Building a Foundation.* Boston: Pearson Education, 2010.

Butterfield, P. M., C. A. Martin, and A. P. Prairie. *Emotional Connections: How Relationships Guide Early Learning.* Washington, DC: Zero to Three, 2004.

Campbell, S. "Caretaking in a Nurturing Way: Replicating Relationship-Based, Reflective Models in Healthy Families Programs." *Zero to Three* 25, no. 5 (May 2005): 17–22.

Center on the Social and Emotional Foundations for Early Learning (CSEFEL). *Using Books to Support Social Emotional Development: Children's Book List*, 2008. http://csefel.vanderbilt.edu/documents/booklist.pdf (accessed November 30, 2010).

Curtis, D., and M. Carter. *Designs for Living and Learning: Transforming Early Childhood Environments.* St. Paul, MN: Redleaf Press, 2003.

Epstein, A. S. *The Intentional Teacher: Choosing the Best Strategies for Young Children's Learning.* Washington, DC: National Association for the Education of Young Children, 2007.

Gilkerson, L., ed., and R. Klein, ed. *Early Development and the Brain: Teaching Resources for Educators.* Washington, DC: Zero to Three, 2008.

Gillespie, L. G., and A. Hunter. "Emotional Flooding—Using Empathy to Help Babies Manage Strong Emotions." *Young Children* 63 (September 2008): 46–47.

Gonzalez-Mena, J. *Multicultural Issues in Child Care.* 2nd ed. Mountain View, CA: Mayfield Publishing, 1997.

Greenspan, S., and N. T. Greenspan. *First Feelings: Milestones in the Emotional Development of Your Baby and Child from Birth to Age 4.* New York: Viking, 1985.

Greenwald, D. "Honoring the Family in Child Care Settings." *Educaring: Resources for Infant Educarers* 31, no. 1 (2010): 1 and 3.

Hohmann, M., and D. P. Weikart. *Educating Young Children.* 2nd ed. Ypsilanti, MI: HighScope Press, 2002.

Honig, A. S. "Infants and Toddlers: Development—The Power of Touch." *Early Childhood Today* 19, no. 5 (March 2005): 25–26.

———. "Outcomes of Infant and Toddler Care." *Montessori Life* 5, no. 4 (Fall 1993): 34–42.

Lally, J. R., and others. *Caring for Infants and Toddlers in Groups: Developmentally Appropriate Practice.* Washington, DC: Zero to Three, 2003.

Lally, J. R., and P. Mangione. "The Uniqueness of Infancy Demands a Responsive Approach to Care." *Young Children* 61, no. 4 (July 2006): 14–20.

Miller, K. "The Most Difficult Transition in Child Care: From the Infant Room into the Toddler Room." *Child Care Information Exchange* 119 (January-February 1998): 88–90.

National Association for the Education of Young Children (NAEYC). http://www.naeyc.org/ (accessed September 10, 2010).

Pawl, J. H., and M. St. John. *How You Are Is as Important as What You Do In Making a Positive Difference for Infants, Toddlers and Their Families.* Washington, DC: Zero to Three, 1998.

Petersen, S., and D. Wittmer. "Relationship-Based Infant Care: Responsive, On Demand, and Predictable." *Young Children* 63, no. 3 (May 2008): 40–42.

Powers, S., ed. "The Developing Mind." *Zero to Three* 28, no. 5 (May 2008):1–48.

Raikes, H. "A Secure Base for Babies: Applying Attachment Concepts to the Infant Care Setting." *Young Children* 51, no. 5 (July 1996): 59–67.

Riley, D., and others. *Social and Emotional Development: Connecting Science and Practice in Early Childhood Settings.* St. Paul, MN: Redleaf Press, 2008.

Endnotes

1. J. Cohen and others, *Helping Young Children Succeed: Strategies to Promote Early Childhood Social and Emotional Development* (Washington, DC: National Conference of State Legislatures and Zero to Three, 2005).

2. National Scientific Council on the Developing Child, *Children's Emotional Development Is Built into the Architecture of Their Brains: Working Paper No. 2* (Winter 2004), p. 2.

3. M. H. Johnson and others, "Newborns' Preferential Tracking of Face-Like Stimuli and Its Subsequent Decline," *Cognition* 40, no. 1–2 (1991): 1–19.

4. A. J. DeCasper and W. P. Fifer, "Of Human Bonding: Newborns Prefer Their Mothers' Voices," *Science* 208, no. 4448 (1980): 1174–76.

5. M. B. Bronson, "Recognizing and Supporting the Development of Self-Regulation in Young Children," *Young Children* 55, no. 2 (2000): 32–37.

6. R. A. Thompson and R. Goodvin, "The Individual Child: Temperament, Emotion, Self and Personality," in *Developmental Science: An Advanced Textbook,* 2nd ed. (Mahwah, NJ: Lawrence Erlbaum Associates, 2005).

7. National Research Council and Institute of Medicine, *From Neurons to Neighborhoods: The Science of Early Childhood Development* (Washington, DC: National Academies Press, 2000), p. 412.

8. J. P. Shonkoff, *Science, Policy, and the Young Developing Child: Closing the Gap Between What We Know and What We Do* (Chicago, IL: Ounce of Prevention Fund, 2004).

9. M. A. Bell and C. D. Wolfe, "Emotion and Cognition: An Intricately Bound Developmental Process," *Child Development* 75, no. 2 (2004): 366.

10. National Research Council and Institute of Medicine, *From Neurons to Neighborhoods: The Science of Early Childhood Development* (Washington, DC: National Academies Press, 2000).

11. J. Panksepp, "The Long-Term Psychobiological Consequences of Infant Emotions: Prescriptions for the Twenty-First Century," *Infant Mental Health Journal* 22, no. 1–2 (2001): 132–73.

12. L. F. Barrett and others, "The Experience of Emotion," *Annual Review of Psychology* 58 (2007): 373–403.

13. Ibid.

14. J. Cohen and others, *Helping Young Children Succeed: Strategies to Promote Early Childhood Social and Emotional Development* (Washington, DC: National Conference of State Legislatures and Zero to Three, 2005).

15. Zero to Three, *Infant and Early Childhood Mental Health: Promoting Healthy Social and Emotional Development* (Washington, DC: Zero to Three, 2004).

16. L. F. Barrett and others, "The Experience of Emotion," *Annual Review of Psychology* 58 (2007): 373–403.

17. National Scientific Council on the Developing Child, *Children's Emotional Development Is Built into the Architecture of Their Brains: Working Paper No. 2* (Winter 2004).

18. C. C. Raver, "Emotions Matter: Making the Case for the Role of Young Children's Emotional Development for Early School Readiness," *Society for Research in Child Development Social Policy Report* 16, no. 3 (2002): 3–19.

19. J. P. Shonkoff, *Science, Policy and the Young Developing Child: Closing the Gap Between What We Know and What We Do* (Chicago, IL: Ounce of Prevention Fund, 2004).

20. California Department of Education, *Infant/Toddler Learning and Development Program Guidelines* (Sacramento: California Department of Education, 2006), p. 25.

21. T. Striano and P. Rochat, "Emergence of Selective Social Referencing in Infancy," *Infancy* 1, no. 2 (2000): 253–64.

22. B. M. Repacholi and A. N. Meltzoff, "Emotional Eavesdropping: Infants Selectively Respond to Indirect Emotional Signals," *Child Development* 78, no. 2 (March/April 2007): 503–21.

23. N. A. Fox and S. D. Calkins, "The Development of Self-Control of Emotion: Intrinsic and Extrinsic Influences," *Motivation and Emotion* 27, no. 1 (2003): 7–26.

24. K. L. Rosenblum, C. J. Dayton, and M. Muzik, "Infant Social and Emotional Development: Emerging Competence in a Relational Context," in *Handbook of Infant Mental Health,* 3rd ed. (New York: Guilford Publishers, 2009).

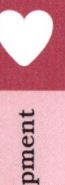

Bibliography

Barrett, L. F., and others. "The Experience of Emotion." *Annual Review of Psychology* 58 (2007): 373–403.

Bell, M. A., and C. D. Wolfe. "Emotion and Cognition: An Intricately Bound Developmental Process." *Child Development* 75, no. 2 (2004): 366–70.

Bronson, M. B. "Recognizing and Supporting the Development of Self-Regulation in Young Children." *Young Children* 55, no. 2 (2000): 32–37.

California Department of Education. *Infant/Toddler Learning and Development Program Guidelines.* Sacramento: California Department of Education, 2006.

Cohen, J., and others. *Helping Young Children Succeed: Strategies to Promote Early Childhood Social and Emotional Development.* Washington, DC: National Conference of State Legislatures and Zero to Three, 2005. http://main.zerotothree.org/site/DocServer/help_yng_child_succeed.pdf?docID=621 (accessed November 24, 2010).

DeCasper, A. J., and W. P. Fifer. "Of Human Bonding: Newborns Prefer Their Mothers' Voices." *Science* 208, no. 4448 (1980): 1174–76.

Fox, N. A., and S. D. Calkins. "The Development of Self-Control of Emotion: Intrinsic and Extrinsic Influences." *Motivation and Emotion* 27, no. 1 (2003): 7–26.

Johnson, M. H., and others. "Newborns' Preferential Tracking of Face-Like Stimuli and Its Subsequent Decline." *Cognition* 40, no. 1–2 (1991): 1–19.

National Research Council and Institute of Medicine. *From Neurons to Neighborhoods: The Science of Early Childhood Development.* Edited by J. P. Shonkoff and D. A. Phillips, Committee on Integrating the Science of Early Childhood Development. Washington, DC: National Academies Press, 2000.

National Scientific Council on the Developing Child. *Children's Emotional Development Is Built into the Architecture of Their Brains: Working Paper No. 2,* Winter 2004. http://developingchild.harvard.edu/index.php/resources/reports_and_working_papers/working_papers/wp2/ (accessed January 27, 2012).

Panksepp, J. "The Long-Term Psychobiological Consequences of Infant Emotions: Prescriptions for the Twenty-First Century." *Infant Mental Health Journal* 22, no. 1–2 (2001): 132–73.

Raver, C. C. "Emotions Matter: Making the Case for the Role of Young Children's Emotional Development for Early School Readiness." *Society for Research in Child Development Social Policy Report* 16, no. 3 (2002): 3–19.

Repacholi, B. M., and A. N. Meltzoff. "Emotional Eavesdropping: Infants Selectively Respond to Indirect Emotional Signals." *Child Development* 78, no. 2 (March/April 2007): 503–21.

Rosenblum, K. L., C. J. Dayton, and M. Muzik. "Infant Social and Emotional Development: Emerging Competence in a Relational Context," in *Handbook of Infant Mental Health.* 3rd ed. Edited by C.H. Zeanah, Jr. New York: Guilford Publishers, 2009.

Shonkoff, J. P. *Science, Policy and the Young Developing Child: Closing the Gap Between What We Know and What We Do.* Chicago, IL: Ounce of Prevention Fund, 2004. http://www.ounceofprevention.org/news/pdfs/Shonkoff.pdf (accessed November 24, 2010).

Striano, T., and P. Rochat. "Emergence of Selective Social Referencing in Infancy." *Infancy* 1, no. 2 (2000): 253–64.

Thompson, R. A., and R. Goodvin. "The Individual Child: Temperament, Emotion, Self and Personality," in *Developmental Science: An Advanced Textbook.* 2nd ed. Edited by M. H. Bornstein and M. E. Lamb. Mahwah, NJ: Lawrence Erlbaum Associates, 2005.

Zero to Three. "Infant and Early Childhood Mental Health: Promoting Healthy Social and Emotional Development." Fact Sheet, May 18, 2004. Washington, DC: Zero to Three, 2004. http://main.zerotothree.org/site/DocServer/Promoting_Social_and_Emotional_Developmentpdf?docID=2081&AddInterest=1144 (accessed January 27, 2012).

Chapter 4
Language Development

> *The acquisition of language and speech seems deceptively simple. Young children learn their mother tongue rapidly and effortlessly, from babbling at six months of age to full sentences by the end of three years, and follow the same developmental path regardless of culture.*
>
> — Patricia K. Kuhl, Ph.D., Professor, Speech and Hearing Sciences, University of Washington[1]

As with all aspects of human development in infancy, language development occurs in the context of relationships. Emotion and language development in the early years are linked, as "much of the form and content of communication between infants and their caregivers in the first year of life depends upon affective expression."[2] The relationship basis of early language development appears right at the beginning of life. Newborns prefer the sounds of their mothers' voices.[3] They also prefer the language spoken by their mothers during pregnancy.[4]

Adults typically modify their speech when communicating with young infants. Research suggests that child-directed speech (also referred to as "parentese" or "motherese") has qualities, notably its pitch or tone and sing-song-like rhythm, which distinguish it from adult-directed speech.[5] Preverbal infants communicate through eye contact, facial expressions, gestures, and sounds. Understanding language precedes using it to communicate.[6] In addition, before being able to use language effectively, infants acquire some understanding of the social processes involved in communication.

They learn about the social aspects of communication by engaging in turn-taking behavior in proto-conversations with their parents or infant care teachers. In proto-conversations, the adult usually says something to the preverbal infant, and the infant responds by making eye contact, cooing, smiling, showing lip and tongue movements, or waving arms. These "conversation-like" exchanges between the adult and infant continue for several turns.

There is broad variability in the pattern and pace of a child's language development.[7] However, the process of early language development is fundamentally the same across cultures and languages. In describing early language development, Kuhl states, "One of the puzzles in language development is to explain the orderly transition that all infants go through during development. Infants the world over achieve certain milestones in linguistic development at roughly the same time, regardless of the language they are exposed to."[8]

Perceptual processes play an important role in language development. As Gogate, Walker-Andrews, and Bahrick note, "A diverse set of experimental findings suggests that early lexical comprehension owes much to infants' developing ability to perceive intersensory relations in auditory–visual events" [for example, speech].[9] A child's experiences also affect language development from a very early age. One of the ways experiences influence language development is through their impact on perception early in infancy. Prior to their first spoken words or word comprehension, infants have already "come to recognize the perceptual properties of their native language."[10] Infants are learning about the prosodic (sound) characteristics of their native language: by nine months of age, English-speaking infants demonstrate a preference for the sound stress pattern characteristic of words in the English language.[11] Kuhl concludes, "At age one—prior to the time infants begin to master higher levels of language, such as sound-meaning correspondences, contrastive phonology, and grammatical rules—infants' perceptual and perceptual-motor systems have been altered by linguistic experience. Phonetic perception has changed dramatically to conform to the native-language pattern, and language-specific speech production has emerged."[12]

Language development naturally occurs through ongoing interactions with adults. Babies have an inborn capacity to learn language that emerges by experiencing language input from adults. Experiences with language allow infants and toddlers to acquire mastery of sounds, grammar, and rules that guide communication and to share meaning with others. By intentionally including language in responsive interactions with infants and toddlers, and by planning experiences that actively engage children in communication, teachers can enrich the complex and amazing process of language development.

Guiding Principles

Be responsive to the active communicator and language learner

Infants and toddlers communicate with adults to express their needs, feelings, and interests. When they initiate communication, they have a clear purpose. Sometimes that purpose is to express a need, and a prompt response from an adult teaches them the power of their communication, helping them become effective communicators. Infants and toddlers also communicate with adults to build their relationships and share meaning. Communication that they initiate to share meaning lasts longer and is more complex. In fact, each moment in which a child initiates communication is a golden opportunity to support the child's learning. Of course, communication during the early months of life is nonverbal. Within the first year of life, the young baby's looks, facial expressions, coos, cries, and sounds are expanded to include parts of words, words, gestures, and pointing. During the first year or so, they engage in back-and-forth, conversation-like exchanges with adults. They may look and smile and then wait for the adult's response. Eventually, the child starts to use simple phrases and sentences to have conversations with familiar adults. At each point in developing the capacity to communicate nonverbally and verbally, responsiveness from adults enhances the child's learning experiences.

Include language in your interactions with infants and toddlers

Experiences with language give the brains of infants and toddlers the necessary input to develop language. Under most circumstances, children experience enough language to gain basic mastery of at least one language. Research indicates that the amount and variety of experiences with communication and language influences children's vocabulary development as well as their general capacity to understand and use language. What is most important is that adults use language when interacting with infants and toddlers. Even when the infant is smiling and cooing, a smile back in response can be enhanced with a statement such as "Oh, what a smile!" A few simple words along with nonverbal communication can make a difference. The exact words are less important than the fact that language is part of the communication with the child. Connecting words with actions, letting a child know what is going to happen next, naming something the child points to—all of this verbal communication engages children in learning language.

Celebrate and support the individual

Although children typically acquire language in more or less the same sequence, they differ from one another in how they go about communicating and learning. For example, a baby with a highly active temperament who tends to approach new situations readily is likely to communicate differently from a child with a quiet temperament who tends to be slow to warm up to new situations. Some children spend a lot of time in "conversation-like" exchanges with their family members and teachers. Others constantly point to things, expecting the adult to say the name. In most cases, different paths to acquiring language lead to the same destination: by around three years of age, the child has basic mastery of one or more languages. Teachers need to observe and become familiar with each child's approach to learning language. Adapting to the individual and being responsive to attempts to share meaning give a strong message of support and encourage the child to continue on her path of communicating, understanding, and using language.

Connect with children's cultural and linguistic experiences at home

The baby's first experiences with language occur at home. From the beginning of life, the child learns the sounds of the family's language or languages and engages in interactions that are rooted in the family's culture. Because the child's home language develops hand in hand with all the other domains, supporting its development is critically important. Differences in early experiences with language and culture are numerous. One difference that often stands out is whether the family emphasizes back-and-forth communication or observational learning during the early months. In some families, adults engage in a lot of face-to-face communication, often relating to the child as an interaction partner. In other families, babies spend a lot of time sitting on someone's lap watching adults communicate. Even so, every culture provides infants and toddlers with a mix of experiences that enable them to learn language and eventually become competent at engaging in conversations. Just as adapting to individual children's paths to learning language is important, so too is connecting with the children's cultural and linguistic experiences at home; doing so can create familiar, meaningful experiences for children in infant/toddler care and can provide a starting point for curriculum planning.

Build on children's interests

As stated in chapter 1, infants and toddlers are active, curious, highly motivated learners. People and things fascinate them. Everything is new to them. They are driven to explore, figure out how things work, and make discoveries. Infants and toddlers enjoy sharing their interests with the adults who care for them. As their capacity to communicate with language grows, children share their sense of wonder and describe their thoughts and interests. Even preverbal infants communicate their interests. A teacher who listens and observes carefully will pick up on a child's interests and gain insights into the child's mind. Understanding the focus of a child's self-initiated learning creates the possibility for making suggestions, asking questions, and posing problems that fuel the child's interests and extends the child's exploration, play, and learning. Moreover, when adults communicate with children about the children's interests, the exchange of ideas lasts longer and is more complex.

Make communication and language interesting and fun

Positive experiences with communication and language motivate infants and toddlers to initiate communication and seek to share meaning with adults. The more fun communication and language are, the better. When teachers become open to the playfulness of infants and toddlers, playful communication becomes part of the relationships with the children. Infants and toddlers love to hear the same song, do the same finger play, and hear the same story over and over again. The excitement children express when they are charmed by playfulness with language is contagious. Teachers feel the children's excitement and enjoy the experience with the children. Repeated engagement in fun and interesting communication promotes children's vocabulary development and their overall capacity to share meaning with others. Discovering the kinds of games and playful interactions that infants and toddlers are drawn to is an integral part of effective curriculum planning in the language development domain.

Create literacy-rich environments

Efforts to foster communication and language development also promote emergent literacy in infants and toddlers. As children learn language, they are building a foundation for later literacy. The connection between language experiences and emergent literacy should be made strong in the infant/toddler curriculum. It is essential to provide a learning environment that offers easily accessible and age-appropriate books. The books

should reflect the experiences of the children and allow for exploration of new images and ideas. Infant/toddler care teachers model the use of books for the children as part of curriculum. When infants indicate an interest in looking at books together with their teachers, it is important for teachers to offer such opportunities regularly. At first, a young infant may show or give teachers books. As children grow older, they may become interested in looking at books and having items labeled by their teachers. The joint attention to books eventually evolves into reading times during which the adult reads and the children listen. In addition to listening, older infants enjoy talking about different aspects of a story. Conversations about books simultaneously promote language development and an interest in literacy.

Summary of the Foundations

The language development domain consists of four foundations:

1. Receptive Language
2. Expressive Language
3. Communication Skills and Knowledge
4. Interest in Print

Please refer to the map of the language development foundations on page 96 for a visual explanation of the terminology used in the infant/toddler learning and development foundations.

Environments and Materials

The environment sets the tone for communication between children and teachers and between children. Infants need places where they can quietly interact with their teachers. In addition, the environment should be arranged to foster communication. It should be easy for teachers to relate with infants at eye level. An important consideration is the number of children in a room or group. Programs that have a policy of maintaining small groups promote the development of close relationships, which enhance both teacher-to-child and child-to-child communication. The following strategies support language development.

Engage infants with books and stories. Experience with books and print in the environment is an important aspect of enhancing early language development and helping infants start on a path of emergent literacy. Children can begin to explore books at an early age, and developing an interest in books builds a strong motivational base for literacy learning in later years.

Moderate background noise. Infants need to be able to hear language in order to develop their capacity to understand and use it. Background noise in the infant/toddler care environment should be moderated through materials that absorb sound and through thoughtful arrangement of equipment. Constant exposure to music and television should be avoided. At times, children are ready to be attentive to music and enjoy it—but if music is playing all the time, it becomes background noise and loses its value in fostering learning.

Arrange the environment to support language development and communication. The environment should be arranged to make it easy for infants to communicate back and forth with adults, look at books and listen to stories from books, engage in finger plays, sing, and participate in other activities.

Provide materials that foster communication. Children tend to be creative with language and practice communicating in personally meaningful ways when they play with open-ended materials such as puppets, blocks, train sets, and dress-up clothes.

Interactions

Infants are naturally attentive to language and, as they grow, actively practice using it. Their inborn capacity to acquire language is activated through communication with adults and other children. At the beginning of life, adults' responses to infants' facial expressions, gaze, vocalizations, and gestures encourage infants to keep trying to communicate their needs and interests. It is important that the adults' responses include both nonverbal signals and language. The amount and quality of language adults use in their communication with infants has a far-reaching impact on infants' language development. The following strategies support language development.

Be responsive when children initiate communication. Responsiveness to an infant's verbalizations, gestures, and communication help him learn that he is a valued conversational partner—that what he wants to communicate is important and of interest. Through responses, a teacher communicates

and models to the child the linguistic, social, and emotional back-and-forth of conversational exchanges. Prompt, appropriate responses signal to the infant an adult's interest in communicating and motivate him to continue in his efforts to communicate.

Engage in nonverbal communication. Spontaneous gestures, facial expressions, and tone of voice communicate meaningful information to infants, who, in turn, often use gestures to communicate prior to being able to use language.

Use child-directed language. Most adults automatically adjust their speech when communicating with young infants, adopting a communication style sometimes called parentese or motherese. This type of speech—which includes adaptations such as a slower pace, higher pitch, repetition, a singsong quality, short sentences, clear pronunciation, grammatically simple sentences, and simple words—makes language more understandable to infants and toddlers.

Use self-talk and parallel talk. Narrating actions while performing them (for example, during caregiving routines) helps infants connect words to the actions and behavior of others. Parallel talk, which consists of adults describing infants' actions or behavior, helps the infants connect their experiences with language.

Help children expand language. Language expansions may include adding words to what the child is expressing through gestures. They may also include building on a child's verbal communication and adding information on a topic of interest. Responding to a child's communication with an open-ended question indicates the listener's interest and gives the child the opportunity to further express herself.

Support dual-language development. Young children who are learning more than one language may learn each language in a somewhat different way. Teachers support the children's developing ability to communicate with family members by conveying respect for each child's home language. Having teachers who speak the home language is the best way to support dual-language development. But if a program has a child whose home language is not spoken by any of the teachers, the program can still create opportunities for the child to hear and use his home language—for example, by inviting volunteers who speak the child's home language to visit the program and by encouraging the volunteers to read, tell stories, sing, and play games in the child's home language.

Attend to individual development and needs. While each child makes progress with language development at her own pace, some children may need additional support to continue making progress and may benefit from early intervention. It is important for teachers to identify potential communication and language-development issues as early as possible in a child's life, by watching for warning signs and referring the child for a comprehensive developmental assessment by a specialist when concerns arise. The California Department of Education and California Department of Developmental Services offer a brochure on this topic, "Reasons for Concern That Your Child or a Child in Your Care May Need Special Help." The brochure is available online at http://www.dds.ca.gov/EarlyStart/docs/ReasonsForConcern_English.pdf (accessed March 19, 2012).

Be playful with language. Rhyming games, finger plays, songs, and pretend play enrich the range of a young child's experiences with language. The rhythm and repetition of a rhyme or song highlight important aspects of language. Playing with language also engages children in positive communication and gives them the message that communicating with language can be fun.

Vignette

It is early in the morning, and 24-month-old Sabela is sitting quietly on the lap of her teacher, Sonja. Sonja and the other teachers talk about the day ahead. Sonja says to another child, "Tony, let's go out early today. It's supposed to rain this morning." Sabela hops up, walks over to the cupboard, and takes out a bag of sand toys to play with outside. Taking out the sand toys and then collecting them to bring them back to the classroom is an activity that Sabela often helps with. Upon seeing Sabela move toward the back door, dragging the sack of sand toys, Sonja makes eye contact and smiles. Sonja also notes that Sabela understood Sonja's comments to Tony.

Responsive Moment

Sabela's teachers have been wondering about her language development. The teachers have documented that Sabela says about 30 different

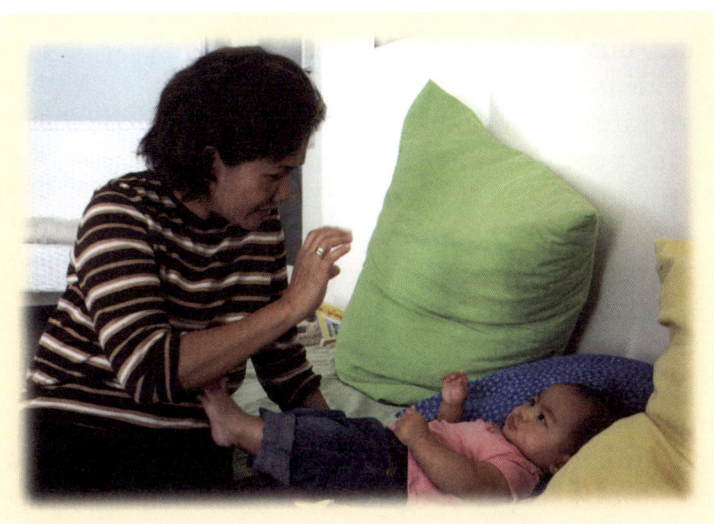

words but is usually quiet and does not engage in conversations. Sabela's father has expressed concern that she is not talking and compares her development to that of her older sister, who is very talkative. Sonja has been watching Sabela closely the past few weeks for indications of language development. When Sabela demonstrated that she understood the discussion about going outside early, Sonja documented that evidence of understanding. Just as important, she acknowledged Sabela's interest in language by offering an encouraging smile.

Vignette

Gustavo, the father of 18-month-old Paula, arrives at Ruth's family child care home in the late afternoon to pick up his daughter. Gustavo sits down so Paula can climb into his lap, and then he greets his daughter in their home language, Portuguese. Ruth sits next to them and says, "Paula, I am going to ask your *Papai* about what you were saying this afternoon." Ruth turns to Gustavo and says, "While we were having lunch, Paula kept saying something that sounded like 'gaffoo.' I felt like she was asking me for something, but I didn't know what it was. Any ideas?" Gustavo asks what they were eating. Ruth tells him they were having pizza. He speaks to Paula in Portuguese, and Paula nods. He grins and says, "I think she was asking for a *garfo*, which is the Portuguese word for 'fork.' At home we eat pizza with a fork." Ruth smiles at Paula and says, "Oh, you wanted a *garfo*—a fork. Next time I will know." Ruth thanks Gustavo and helps him prepare Paula to leave for the day.

Responsive Moment

Ruth wants to support Paula's development of both Portuguese and English, so she has learned a few Portuguese words from the family to use with Paula during care routines and play. Paula has recently started to talk a lot, and Ruth has observed that many of Paula's words are in Portuguese. By reaching out to Gustavo and asking for his help, Ruth increased her knowledge and her ability to support Paula's home language and culture. In this particular situation, Ruth learned a new word to use with Paula and gained some insight into the family's mealtime routine. Additionally, the interaction among the three of them at the end of the day allowed Ruth to strengthen her relationship with the family.

Research Highlight 1

Infants come into the world as universal language learners, able to distinguish sounds from all over the world equally well. It is not until between approximately nine and 12 months of age that an infant's language capacities become specific to the language that the infant has heard in her or his everyday language environment. For example, in a study conducted with American and Japanese infants, at seven months of age, both Japanese and American infants were able to discriminate between the sounds /l/ and /r/. However, by 11 months, Japanese infants had much greater difficulty making this distinction, whereas American infants retained the capacity to discriminate between these two sounds.[13] In the Japanese language, /r/ and /l/ are perceived as one sound, whereas in English they are separate sounds. Similarly, studies have shown that capacity of monolingual English-speaking infants to discriminate specific sounds in Spanish and Mandarin declines at around 12 months of age.[14, 15] Recent brain research further suggests that an infant's brain commits neural pathways to perceiving language-specific speech patterns based upon exposure to communication in the infant's native language.[16]

Research Highlight 2

Infants learn language through back-and-forth exchanges with parents and other adults who provide care for them. Specifically, research suggests that mothers who respond contingently to infants' vocalizations promote both more frequent and higher-quality vocalizations than those who respond in less contingent ways.[17] In addition to children's experiences at home, research on young children's experiences in child care suggests that sensitive, responsive, and stimulating caregiving interactions predict positive language-development outcomes (e.g., vocabulary and grammar) for young children. The interactions that mothers and child care providers have with children make important and unique contributions to children's language-development outcomes.[18]

Sample Developmental Sequences

Expressive Language (communication of needs, feelings, and interests)

Definition: As children develop, they use language to communicate nonverbally and verbally to express their needs, feelings, and interests.

Beginning level: Children make sounds spontaneously. For instance, they cry or coo.

Next level: Children use gestures, sounds, or facial expressions to communicate needs, feelings, and interests. For example, they wave arms or kick legs excitedly when an adult blows bubbles, or they cry when hungry.

Next level: Children have a few special words or gestures to communicate needs, feelings, and interests. For instance, a child may ask a teacher for a blanket by using her special word or gesture for "blanket."

Next level: Children use a variety of simple words or gestures to communicate needs, feelings, and interests. For example, they may play with the meaning of the word "no" or they may say that they want a cookie and then take a cookie from the plate.

Next level: Children use simple combinations of words to communicate needs, feelings, and interests. For instance, they may say "More juice" when thirsty.

Next level: Children communicate in a way that is understandable to most adults who speak the same language they do. They combine words into phrases or sentences and demonstrate the ability to follow some grammatical rules of the home language. For example, they might say, "Me go outside," "I want my mommy," or "I don't like that."

Interest in Print (interest in literacy)

Definition: Children show interest in books, songs, rhymes, finger plays, and stories. As children grow older, many of their everyday activities relate

to an interest in print—for example, making intentional marks on paper with a crayon or marker, pretending to read and write, repeating stories and rhymes, recognizing images in books, noticing common symbols and words, and enjoying books. Interest in print can be considered one aspect of emergent literacy (the idea that literacy starts to develop during early childhood, well before a child enters school).[19]

Beginning level: Children respond to books and songs. For instance, they quiet themselves when an adult sings a song, or they look at a book when the adult holds it in their field of vision.

Next level: Children play with books and respond to songs. For example, they may touch or squeeze vinyl or cloth book covers or coo when adult sings.

Next level: Children attend for a short period of time as an adult reads books, sings songs, or says rhymes. They explore books and show interest in literacy activities, such as looking at photos and books with an adult. For instance, they will try to turn the page of a board book as the adult talks about pictures on the page, or they will listen to simple songs or rhymes and do one basic hand motion with song.

Next level: Children choose to participate in reading, singing, or rhyming initiated by the adult. They actively notice print in the environment. For example, they may sit next to a teacher who is reading to another child and ask simple questions (such as "What's that?") when being read to.

Next level: Children initiate and show appreciation for reading, listening to stories, imitating rhymes, and singing songs. For instance, they may ask the teacher to tell a story or sing a song; bring the teacher a favorite book in order to be read to; or make scribble marks on paper and pretend to read what they scribbled.

Engaging Families

Working together, families and early education programs provide critical support for young children's language development. During the first three years of life, the focus should be on communication that includes language, having fun with language, and laying the foundation for future language and literacy development through developmentally appropriate and culturally and linguistically inclusive experiences rather than on the acquisition of discrete skills. Infant care teachers can build on children's language experiences in the home and, at the same time, share with families what is being done in group care to enhance language learning.

- Ask family members to provide a list of words children know in their home language (or words that are specific to the child or the family), including the names or titles of family members, pets, friends, neighbors, and so on. Share words that children have learned through various experiences in the early education setting and, if necessary, consider providing home-language translations of words that children are acquiring in English.

- Create a lending library so that families can take home books and other reading materials, available in English and in the families' home languages, to enjoy with their children during evening hours and on the weekends.

- When participating in interactions with infants, toddlers, and their families, acknowledge the communication efforts of all children by commenting on their use of nonverbal gestures, body movements, facial expressions, and vocalizations.

- Bathe infants and toddlers in language by engaging in "extra" talk that goes beyond the business of daily living; for example, play with sounds, sing, or make up nonsense words together.

2. In addition to supporting language acquisition, what are some other benefits that result when infant care teachers become familiar with the words that young children use to describe important people in their lives, significant events, and places?

3. How might regular observation of children's language development in different contexts (e.g., during quiet activities, outdoors, during mealtimes) and with different social partners (e.g., familiar and unfamiliar adults and peers) help you understand children's language and foster your communication with their families?

Questions for Reflection

1. What nonverbal gestures and facial expressions do infants and toddlers in your program make, and how can you incorporate their communications into back-and-forth interactions with them? What are some individual differences you have observed in children's use of verbal or nonverbal language?

Concluding Thoughts

Among the many developing capacities of infants and toddlers, language development is one of the most amazing. Children's capacity for learning language relies on experiencing language in their interactions with adults. By planning environments that encourage communication and by being intentional in their communications with infants and toddlers, infant care teachers can strengthen children's language development. Perhaps the most important thing that teachers can do is include language in their interactions with children. By listening to and observing children, and learning from families about children's communication experiences at home, teachers can understand each child's path to learning language—and they share meaning with children by engaging in responsive communication with each child.

Map of the Foundations

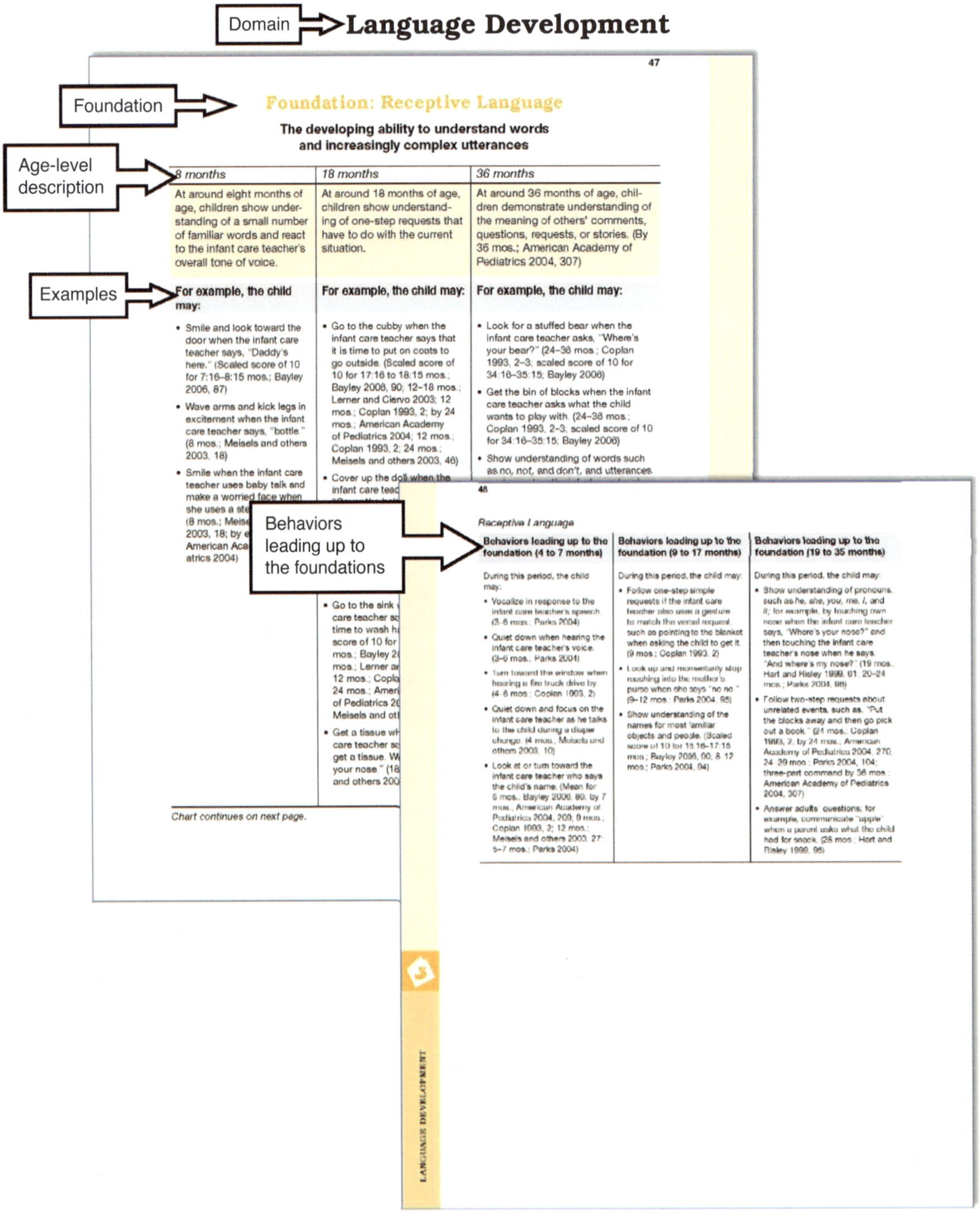

Domain → Language Development

Foundation → Foundation: Receptive Language
The developing ability to understand words and increasingly complex utterances

Age-level description →

8 months	18 months	36 months
At around eight months of age, children show understanding of a small number of familiar words and react to the infant care teacher's overall tone of voice.	At around 18 months of age, children show understanding of one-step requests that have to do with the current situation.	At around 36 months of age, children demonstrate understanding of the meaning of others' comments, questions, requests, or stories. (By 36 mos.; American Academy of Pediatrics 2004, 307)

Examples → For example, the child may:

- Smile and look toward the door when the infant care teacher says, "Daddy's here." (Scaled score of 10 for 7:16–8:15 mos.; Bayley 2006, 87)
- Wave arms and kick legs in excitement when the infant care teacher says, "bottle." (8 mos.; Meisels and others 2003, 18)
- Smile when the infant care teacher uses baby talk and make a worried face when she uses a stern [tone] (8 mos.; Meisels 2003, 18; by [6 mos.] American Academy of Pediatrics 2004)

For example, the child may:

- Go to the cubby when the infant care teacher says that it is time to put on coats to go outside. (Scaled score of 10 for 17:16 to 18:15 mos.; Bayley 2006, 90; 12–18 mos.; Lerner and Ciervo 2003; 12 mos.; Coplan 1993, 2; by 24 mos.; American Academy of Pediatrics 2004; 12 mos.; Coplan 1993, 2; 24 mos.; Meisels and others 2003, 46)
- Cover up the doll when the infant care teach[er...]

For example, the child may:

- Look for a stuffed bear when the infant care teacher says, "Where's your bear?" (24–36 mos.; Coplan 1993, 2–3; scaled score of 10 for 34:16–35:15; Bayley 2006)
- Get the bin of blocks when the infant care teacher asks what the child wants to play with. (24–36 mos.; Coplan 1993, 2–3, scaled score of 10 for 34:16–35:15; Bayley 2006)
- Show understanding of words such as *no*, *not*, and *don't*, and utterances

Behaviors leading up to the foundations →

Receptive Language

Behaviors leading up to the foundation (4 to 7 months)	Behaviors leading up to the foundation (9 to 17 months)	Behaviors leading up to the foundation (19 to 35 months)
During this period, the child may: • Vocalize in response to the infant care teacher's speech. (3–6 mos.; Parks 2004) • Quiet down when hearing the infant care teacher's voice. (3–6 mos.; Parks 2004) • Turn toward the window when hearing a fire truck drive by. (4–6 mos.; Coplan 1993, 2) • Quiet down and focus on the infant care teacher as he talks to the child during a diaper change. (4 mos.; Meisels and others 2003, 10) • Look at or turn toward the infant care teacher who says the child's name. (Mean for 6 mos.; Bayley 2006, 80; by 7 mos.; American Academy of Pediatrics 2004, 209; 9 mos.; Coplan 1993, 2; 12 mos.; Meisels and others 2003, 27; 5–7 mos.; Parks 2004)	During this period, the child may: • Follow one-step simple requests if the infant care teacher also uses a gesture to match the verbal request such as pointing to the blanket when asking the child to get it. (9 mos.; Coplan 1993, 2) • Look up and momentarily stop reaching into the mother's purse when she says "no no." (9–12 mos.; Parks 2004, 95) • Show understanding of the names for most familiar objects and people. (Scaled score of 10 for 16:16–17:15 mos.; Bayley 2006, 90; 8–12 mos.; Parks 2004, 94)	During this period, the child may: • Show understanding of pronouns, such as *he*, *she*, *you*, *me*, *I*, and *it*; for example, by touching own nose when the infant care teacher says, "Where's your nose?" and then touching the infant care teacher's nose when he says, "And where's my nose?" (19 mos.; Hart and Risley 1999, 91; 20–24 mos.; Parks 2004, 98) • Follow two-step requests about unrelated events, such as, "Put the blocks away and then go pick out a book." (24 mos.; Coplan 1993, 2; by 24 mos.; American Academy of Pediatrics 2004, 270; 24–29 mos.; Parks 2004, 104; three-part command by 36 mos.; American Academy of Pediatrics 2004, 307) • Answer adults' questions; for example, communicate "apple" when a parent asks what the child had for snack. (28 mos.; Hart and Risley 1999, 95)

Chart continues on next page.

Teacher Resources

American Speech-Language-Hearing Association. "Learning Two Languages." http://www.asha.org/public/speech/development/BilingualChildren.htm (accessed March 20, 2012).

Bowman, B., ed. *Love to Read: Essays in Developing and Enhancing Early Literacy Skills of African American Children.* Washington, DC: National Black Child Development Institute, Inc., 2002.

Brown, D. K. The Children's Literature Web Guide, 1994–2001. http://people.ucalgary.ca/~dkbrown/ (accessed September 10, 2010).

California Association for Bilingual Education (CABE). http://www.bilingualeducation.org/ (accessed September 7, 2010).

California Department of Education. *Preschool English Learners: Principles and Practices to Promote Language, Literacy, and Learning.* 2nd ed. Sacramento: California Department of Education, 2009.

Curtis, D. "Can Babies Read and Write?" *Childcare Information Exchange* 31, no. 188 (July/August 2009): 42–43.

Deiner, Penny L. *Infants and Toddlers: Development and Curriculum Planning.* 2nd ed. Clifton Park, NY: Delmar Cengage Learning, 2009.

Espinosa, L. *Challenging Common Myths About Young English Language Learners.* Foundation for Child Development Policy Brief, no. 8, January 2008. http://www.fcd-us.org/resources/resources-show.htm?doc_id=669789 (accessed September 7, 2010).

HighScope Educational Research Foundation. HighScope: Inspiring Educators to Inspire Children, 2009. http://www.highscope.org/ (accessed September 10, 2010).

National Early Literacy Panel, National Center for Family Literacy, and National Institute for Literacy. *Developing Early Literacy: Report of the National Early Literacy Panel: A Scientific Synthesis of Early Literacy Development and Implications for Intervention.* Jessup, MD: National Institute for Literacy at ED Pubs, 2008.

NICHD Early Child Care Research Network and A. Clarke-Stewart. "A New Guide for Evaluating Child Care Quality." *Zero to Three* 21, no. 5 (April/May 2001): 40–47.

Soto, L. D. *Language, Culture, and Power: Bilingual Families and the Struggle for Quality Education.* Albany, NY: State University of New York Press, 1997.

Swim, T. *Infants and Toddlers.* Clifton Park, NY: Thomson Delmar Learning, 2007.

Wittmer, D. S., and S. H. Petersen. *Infant and Toddler Development and Responsive Program Planning: A Relationship-Based Approach.* 2nd ed. Upper Saddle River, NJ: Pearson Education, Inc., 2010.

Zambo, D., and C. C. Hansen. "Love, Language, and Emergent Literacy: Pathways to Emotional Development of the Very Young." *Young Children* 62, no. 3 (May 2007): 32–37.

Endnotes

1. P. K. Kuhl, "Early Language Acquisition: Cracking the Speech Code," *Nature Reviews Neuroscience* 5 (2004): 831.

2. L. Bloom and J. Capatides, "Expression of Affect and the Emergence of Language," *Child Development* 58 (1987): 1513.

3. A. DeCasper and W. Fifer, "On Human Bonding: Newborns Prefer Their Mothers' Voices," *Science* 208 (1980): 1174–76.

4. C. Moon, R. Cooper, and W. Fifer, "Two-Day-Olds Prefer their Native Language," *Infant Behavior and Development* 16 (1993): 495–500.

5. R. P. Cooper and others, "The Development of Infants' Preference for Motherese," *Infant Behavior and Development* 20, no. 4 (1997): 477–88.

6. L. Bloom and others, "Early Conversations and Word Learning: Contributions from Child and Adult," *Child Development* 67 (1996): 3154–75.

7. L. Bloom and J. Capatides, "Expression of Affect and the Emergence of Language," *Child Development* 58 (1987): 1513–22.

8. P. K. Kuhl, "Speech, Language and Developmental Change," in *Emerging Cognitive Abilities in Early Infancy*. Edited by F. Lacerda, C. von Hofsten, and M. Heimann (Mahwah, NJ: Lawrence Erlbaum Associates, 2002), p. 115.

9. L. Gogate, A. Walker-Andrews, and L. Bahrick, "The Intersensory Origins of Word Comprehension: An Ecological-Dynamic Systems View," *Developmental Science* 4, no. 1 (2001): 13.

10. P. K. Kuhl, "Speech, Language and Developmental Change," in *Emerging Cognitive Abilities in Early Infancy*. Edited by F. Lacerda, C. von Hofsten, and M. Heimann (Mahwah, NJ: Lawrence Erlbaum Associates, 2002), p. 19.

11. J. Jusczyk, A. Cutler, and N. J. Redanz, "Infants' Preference for the Predominant Stress Patterns of English Words," *Child Development* 64 (1993): 675–87.

12. P. K. Kuhl, "Speech, Language and Developmental Change," in *Emerging Cognitive Abilities in Early Infancy*. Edited by F. Lacerda, C. von Hofsten, and M. Heimann (Mahwah, NJ: Lawrence Erlbaum Associates, 2002), p. 112.

13. G. Whitehurst and C. Lonigan, "Child Development and Emergent Literacy," *Child Development* 69, no. 3 (1998): 848–72.

14. M. River-Gaxiola, J. Silva-Pereyra, and P. K. Kuhl, "Brain Potentials to Native and Non-native Speech Contrasts in Seven- and Eleven-Month-Old American infants," *Developmental Science* 8, no. 2 (2005): 162–72.

15. P. K. Kuhl, F-M. Tsao, and H-M. Liu, "Foreign-language Experience in Infancy: Effects of Short-term Exposure and Social Interaction on Phonetic Learning," *Proceedings of the National Academy of Sciences of the United States of America* 100, no. 15 (July 2003): 9096–9101.

16. P. K. Kuhl, "Early Language Acquisition: Cracking the Speech Code," *Nature Reviews Neuroscience* 5 (2004): 831.

17. M. Goldstein, A. King, and M. West, "Social Interaction Shapes Babbling: Testing Parallels Between Birdsong and Speech," *Proceedings of the National Academy of Sciences of the United States of America* 100, no.13 (2003): 8030–35.

18. K. Hirsh-Pasek and M. Burchinal, "Mother and Caregiver Sensitivity Over Time: Predicting Language and Academic Outcomes with Variable- and Person-centered Approaches," *Merrill-Palmer Quarterly* 52, no. 3 (July 2006): 449–85.

19. G. Whitehurst and C. Lonigan, "Child Development and Emergent Literacy," *Child Development* 69, no. 3 (1998): 848–72.

Bibliography

Bloom, L., and J. Capatides. "Expression of Affect and the Emergence of Language." *Child Development* 58 (1987): 1513–22.

Bloom, L., and others. "Early Conversations and Word Learning: Contributions from Child and Adult." *Child Development* 67 (1996): 3154–75.

Cooper, R. P., and others. "The Development of Infants' Preference for Motherese." *Infant Behavior and Development* 20, no. 4 (1997): 477–88.

DeCasper, A., and W. Fifer. "On Human Bonding: Newborns Prefer Their Mothers' Voices." *Science* 208 (1980): 1174–76.

Gogate, L., A. Walker-Andrews, and L. Bahrick. "The Intersensory Origins of Word Comprehension: An Ecological-Dynamic Systems View." *Developmental Science* 4, no. 1 (2001): 1–37.

Goldstein, M., A. King, and M. West. "Social Interaction Shapes Babbling: Testing Parallels Between Birdsong and Speech." *Proceedings of the National Academy of Sciences of the United States of America* 100, no.13 (2003): 8030–35.

Hirsh-Pasek, K., and M. Burchinal. "Mother and Caregiver Sensitivity Over Time: Predicting Language and Academic Outcomes with Variable- and Person-centered Approaches." *Merrill-Palmer Quarterly* 52, no. 3 (July 2006): 449–85.

Jusczyk, J., A. Cutler, and N. J. Redanz. "Infants' Preference for the Predominant Stress Patterns of English Words." *Child Development* 64 (1993): 675–87.

Kuhl, P. K. "Early Language Acquisition: Cracking the Speech Code." *Nature Reviews Neuroscience* 5 (2004): 831–43.

———. "Speech, Language and Developmental Change," in *Emerging Cognitive Abilities in Early Infancy*. Edited by F. Lacerda, C. von Hofsten, and M. Heimann. Mahwah, NJ: Lawrence Erlbaum Associates, 2002.

Kuhl, P. K., and others. "Infants Show a Facilitation for Native Language Phonetic Perception Between 6 and 12 months." *Developmental Science* 9, no. 2 (2006): F13–F21.

Kuhl, P. K., F-M. Tsao, and H-M. Liu. "Foreign-language Experience in Infancy: Effects of Short-term Exposure and Social Interaction on Phonetic Learning." *Proceedings of the National Academy of Sciences of the United States of America* 100, no. 15 (July 2003): 9096–9101.

Moon, C., R. Cooper, and W. Fifer. "Two-Day-Olds Prefer their Native Language." *Infant Behavior and Development* 16 (1993): 495–500.

River-Gaxiola, M., J. Silva-Pereyra, and P. K. Kuhl. "Brain Potentials to Native and Non-native Speech Contrasts in Seven- and Eleven-Month-Old American infants." *Developmental Science* 8, no. 2 (2005): 162–72.

Whitehurst, G., and C. Lonigan. "Child Development and Emergent Literacy." *Child Development* 69, no. 3 (1998): 848–72.

Chapter 5
Cognitive Development

> [P]sychologists and neuroscientists have discovered that babies not only learn more, but imagine more, care more, and experience more than we would ever have thought possible. In some ways, young children are actually smarter, more imaginative, more caring, and even more conscious than adults are.
>
> — Alison Gopnik, in *The Philosophical Baby: What Children's Minds Tell Us About Truth, Love, and the Meaning of Life*[1]

The term *cognitive development* refers to the process of growth and change in intellectual or mental abilities such as thinking, reasoning, and understanding. It includes the acquisition and consolidation of knowledge. Over the past three decades, infancy research has caused developmental psychologists to change the way they characterize the earliest stages of cognitive development. Once regarded as an organism driven mainly by simple sensorimotor schemes, the infant is now seen as having sophisticated cognitive skills and concepts that guide knowledge acquisition.[2]

Infants draw on social–emotional, language, and perceptual and motor experiences and abilities for cognitive development. They are attuned to relationships between characteristics of objects, actions, and the physical environment. They are particularly attuned to people. Family members, friends, and teachers play an essential role in supporting the cognitive development of infants by providing the healthy interpersonal and social–emotional context in which cognitive development unfolds. Caring, responsive adults provide the base from which infants can fully engage in behaviors and interactions that promote learning. Such adults also serve as a prime source for imitation.

Cultural context is important in young children's cognitive development. There is substantial variation in how intelligence is defined within different cultures.[3] As a result, different aspects of cognitive performance may be more highly valued in some cultural contexts than in others. For example, processing speed is an aspect of intelligence that is highly valued in some cultures, whereas in other cultures, adjectives such as *slow, careful,* and *active* may be more associated with intelligence.[4] Likewise, in some cultural contexts, aspects of intelligence that have to do with social competence appear to be seen as more important than speed.[5] It is crucial for early childhood educators to recognize the role that cultural context plays in defining and setting the stage for children's healthy cognitive functioning.

Research has identified a broad range of cognitive competencies and described the remarkable progression of cognitive development during the early childhood years. Experts in the field describe infants as active, motivated, and engaged learners who possess an impressive range of cognitive competencies and learn through exploration.[6, 7] Infants exhibit natural curiosity.[8] They have a strong drive to learn, and their actions reflect that drive. Indeed, they have been described as "born to learn."[9]

To optimize early cognitive development, infant/toddler care teachers need to establish relationships that provide infants and toddlers with a secure base for exploration and discovery. Infants and toddlers thrive in environments that offer a mix of novelty, familiarity, and appropriate challenges. They actively learn through interacting with adults and other children and imitating them. Above all, their natural curiosity and drive to learn grow through the responsiveness and encouragement of caring adults.

Guiding Principles

Relate to the child as an active meaning maker

Infants and toddlers actively seek to make sense of every experience they have. The sound of keys in the door may inspire pleasure or fear, depending on what the child may have learned to expect when the door opens. Repeated experiences lead to expectations that become meaningful for the child. For instance, when a young infant is regularly held securely in the arms of an adult who is attentive and makes soothing noises, the child may associate that adult's presence with

comfort and a feeling of security. Over time, the mere sight or sound of that same adult may help the child feel safe and nurtured, even before the adult approaches the child. By being responsive to the infant's active engagement with the social and physical world, teachers create experiences together with the child and share meaning, which is a key part of adult–infant relationships.

Provide opportunities for exploration

Through responsive interactions and thoughtful selection of materials, teachers provide opportunities for children to explore and make discoveries. Infants and toddlers learn about the world through play, exploration, and interactions. They explore the relationship between cause and effect, identify the permanence of objects, experiment with tools, develop an understanding of spatial relationships, and learn by imitating the behaviors of other people. Observing children's exploration leads to new possibilities. For example, a teacher who observes a child banging objects on various surfaces may then provide new and different objects that the child may also pick up and bang. Each object offers different sensorimotor experiences; for example, each makes a different sound when banged or changes shape and feels different when pressure is applied. Rather than banging the new objects, the child may mouth them or crawl right past them. Each of the child's actions becomes an opportunity for the teacher to continue to observe and wonder about the child's interests. The teacher provides an environment and materials rich with possibilities for exploration and

then is a supportive, responsive presence as the child explores and learns.

Respect the child's initiative and choices

Infants and toddlers demonstrate initiative when they play, explore, and interact. Caring adults can "tune in" to each child by paying close attention to gaze, body movements, facial expressions, and vocalizations. In each moment, the child is taking initiative and making choices. Imagine an eight-month-old child on a changing table. His teacher is helping him put on a clean shirt. The teacher holds out the left sleeve, but the child puts out his right arm rather than his left one. In this moment, the teacher can acknowledge and respect the child's initiative to participate in the routine by thanking him and switching to the left sleeve. This simple adaptation by the teacher lets the child know that the teacher values his initiative. Sensitive teachers use moments like this one to encourage children's initiative and choices and build cooperative relationships with the children.

Allow ample time for children to make sense of experiences

Time is a gift. The infant/toddler program can be for children and families a sanctuary in which the world slows down, giving them time to look, listen, think, feel, and enjoy each other. Allowing children ample time to explore, to participate in interactions and care routines, and to make sense of experiences supports their learning. Children usually need more time than adults to solve a problem, make a discovery, test an idea, observe another person, and transition from one place or activity to another. When teachers create a relaxed, unhurried pace in the child care setting, infants and toddlers can take the time they need to concentrate on their interests and fully experience feelings. A toddler who has fallen may remain on the ground (or floor) for a while, lying down, crying, wondering what happened, feeling angry or hurt. Rather than rushing in and picking up the child, a teacher may crouch low, place a hand on the child, and offer comfort while allowing the child time to gather herself together. All children need time, but each may use it differently. One may want to get right into the teacher's lap, while another may want to stay where he is for a while. Allowing children to set the pace whenever possible gives them the opportunity to practice developing skills and to learn about their interests, needs, and abilities.

Appreciate the child's creativity

Infants and toddlers often approach a new opportunity with a fresh perspective. They may find alternative ways to relate to play materials and other objects. For example, puzzle pieces may be collected in a basket, or a chair may be used as a climber or a changing table for a baby doll. A young toddler's first experience with play dough may include taking a little taste, as the child may not know how to use this dough but may have seen food with a similar appearance and texture at the eating table. In every situation, teachers have a primary responsibility to keep children safe and establish rules to ensure their safety. But when a child's explorations lead her to use materials in a novel, unexpected way—for example, climbing up a slide or wearing a purse as a hat—

such actions can be a creative form of learning rather than mistakes. It is important for teachers to appreciate the openness and curiosity of a child's mind even when they have to set limits for the child. The infant's curiosity and drive to learn are fueled by the freedom to be creative in a challenging yet safe learning environment.

Describe the child's actions and the effects of actions

Infants and toddlers learn by exploring and manipulating objects and by interacting with others. Things that may be obvious to adults can be completely new and fascinating to infants and toddlers. They learn about the properties of an object, such as how it rolls, bounces, or clicks together with similar objects. They also learn that it may be okay to move past a certain child on a climbing structure, but another child may push when being passed. This learning happens through active navigation of the environment, exploration, manipulation of objects, and experimentation. Teachers can support self-initiated learning by describing the child's actions. A statement such as, "You ate all of the peas on your plate, and now the plate is empty" acknowledges the outcome of the child's action and gives information to the child. It lets the child know that the teacher is attentive and cares about him. The teacher's comments may also illuminate a concept for a child, such as the difference between *full* and *empty*. Teacher comments that acknowledge the meaning of an infant's or toddler's actions create both an emotional and intellectual connection with the child.

Support self-initiated repetition and practice

Infants and toddlers often repeat actions. This self-initiated repetition strengthens their learning. They may repeat an action, such as mouthing an object or sliding an object back and forth, to gather information. They may practice pulling themselves up to stand or repeatedly grasp and turn the dial on a toy. Their interest in repetition and practice also extends to their relationships with adults. For example, infants and toddlers may ask an adult to read the same book or sing the same song over and over. As often as possible, adults should support this interest in repetition, as it reflects children's drive to learn and helps them gain mastery of new knowledge and skills. Daily routines such as

meals and naps will necessarily interrupt self-initiated learning, but during play times, infants and toddlers benefit from having ample time and opportunities to practice and repeat.

Give appropriate encouragement for problem solving and mastery

Knowing when to help, when to stand back, and when to encourage are skills that a teacher develops over time. For infants and toddlers, sharing a moment of mastery with an adult can affirm their interest in making a discovery or mastering a new skill. A nearby adult who gives attention while allowing the child to work on a problem encourages the child to continue exploring and trying. A teacher who sits nearby and does not interrupt or interfere with the child communicates confidence in the child's ability to handle a situation. The teacher gives the message, "I am here if you need me, but I think you can handle it." For instance, if an infant is intently pulling on the short cord of a toy phone, concentrating, perhaps even grunting, a teacher may come close, watch, and comment, "I see you pulling on that phone." When the child pulls the toy phone into her lap, the teacher may say, "You got it!" The child may look up at the teacher, make eye contact, and smile or may continue to play with confidence and ease. No matter how infants and toddlers respond, encouragement that gives them time and space for exploration and problem solving boosts their capacity to learn.

Support the child's active participation in personal care routines

During personal care routines such as diapering, feeding or eating, dressing, and even wiping a nose, infants and toddlers can participate actively. Routines usually consist of a sequence of events. For instance, the steps one follows with handwashing—turning on the water, getting soap, washing, rinsing, and drying hands—happen in the same order each time. The predictable nature of care routines provides an excellent opportunity for infants and toddlers to participate and to anticipate the next step. Upon arriving at the sink, the child may reach out to turn on the water, or, after rinsing, turn to tug on the paper towels. When routines are predictable and performed by a consistent primary care teacher, the infant or toddler and the teacher can develop understandings and share meaning with each other. For example, a child and an adult who often participate in routines together may take turns doing certain actions or may assign roles in carrying out the routine. Over time, consistently practicing care routines with an infant or toddler allows the teacher to observe and adapt as the child learns and as her level of participation develops.

Summary of the Foundations

The cognitive development domain consists of 10 foundations:

1. Cause-and-Effect
2. Spatial Relationships
3. Problem Solving
4. Imitation
5. Memory
6. Number Sense
7. Classification
8. Symbolic Play

9. Attention Maintenance
10. Understanding of Personal Care Routines

Please refer to the map of the cognitive development foundations on page 119 for a visual explanation of the terminology used in the infant/toddler learning and development foundations.

Environments and Materials

Thoughtfully selecting play materials and making them available to children in well-organized play spaces are primary components of infant/toddler curriculum. By carefully creating play spaces that include toys matched to the children's observed interests, teachers support each child's strong drive to build knowledge through active exploration. The following strategies promote cognitive development in infants and toddlers.

Provide play spaces with rich opportunities for learning. Carefully consider the placement and quality of play materials. Set up spaces where infants can play without being disturbed by adult traffic. Once infants are mobile and can search for toys, divide the play space into distinct areas, each with an identity—that is, areas where play materials of a particular type can be found. For example, teachers might arrange books, laminated photos, puppets, and stuffed dolls and animals in a corner along with comfortable seating where the teacher and infants can read or tell stories together. A low shelf can be used as a divider to create a play nook for cause-and-effect toys. Another area might be set up for active movement—for example, pulling to stand up, cruising, climbing, balancing, and sliding.

Keep toys in places that are easily visible and accessible. Low baskets (wide-woven or plastic) and clear plastic bins are easy for infants to see and allow the children to select play materials readily.

Consider both novelty and predictability when preparing the environment. Infants enjoy searching for favorite and familiar toys. Finding familiar items gives them a sense of predictability and competence, the

feeling of "I know this!" or "I know where to find that." They also enjoy new objects—ones that are sufficiently similar to be inviting yet sufficiently different to pique their curiosity. Provide a basic selection of toys each day, and store the toys in consistent, predictable locations in both the indoor and outdoor play environments; this will help the infants know where to find particular toys. Add new items to the play areas on a regular basis to support the children's curiosity. However, be mindful to maintain a balance between familiarity and novelty. Give infants and toddlers ample time to become familiar with a thoughtfully selected collection of toys. If the toys are changed too often, the children's play becomes superficial rather than complex and engaging. On the other hand, when infants stop playing with certain toys, it is time for teachers to remove the all-too-familiar play materials from the learning environment. The goal should be to offer a sufficient quantity of engaging materials in the play space, some that are known and some that are novel. Above all, the rotation of play materials in and out of the environment should be based on careful observation of infants' play rather than on a predetermined schedule.

Arrange the environment to encourage exploration. Crawling infants and young toddlers move toys from place to place. As a result, the floor is often strewn with toys in the wake of their exploration and movement. This is normal. Be mindful that when toys are scattered far from their designated storage areas, infants' exploration might be interrupted or stopped. Periodically pass through the play space to return to their storage areas items that have been cast aside. This practice keeps the play space inviting and the toys accessible to the infants. Arrange some of the toys in an interesting way to engage and extend the mind of the curious toddler. For example, if a group of young toddlers is fascinated with filling containers and then emptying them (often by dumping the contents), place small items around several containers that are just the right size for filling and emptying. Or, based on observations of the mode of play or the types of toys being used, add new items that engage such play in a similar or a more complex way. Infants who are not yet able to roll over and search for desired toys rely on teachers to help them gain possession of things. Until infants begin to move on their own from place to place, teachers prepare the play space with a few items that are within the infants' grasp. Once the infants begin to roll and crawl, teachers prepare the entire play space with toys that attract the increasingly mobile infants.

Offer toys that support an understanding of spatial relationships through nesting and stacking. As infants connect toys in various ways, they discover a special property: that objects can be nested inside each other or stacked to become longer or taller. When placing one object inside another (e.g., conical plastic cups, baskets, bins, sand pails, or hollow blocks), infants explore relative size and how things fit in space. When stacking such objects, placing them side by side or on top of one another, infants discover how to construct horizontal lines and vertical towers. Toddlers independently invent patterns with objects that nest and are multicolored, arranging a particular color to appear in a certain location—at the bottom, the top, or in the middle. As they explore nesting, toddlers discover that, based on similarities and differences in size and shape, some objects fit together and others do not. They also explore volume as they discover that an object having the same shape as another, smaller object can contain the smaller object. With repeated practice they learn to tell, simply by looking at objects, which ones will allow them to perform stacking or nesting and which ones will not.

Offer toys that support cause-and-effect experimentation. At 18 months of age, toddlers enjoy the challenge of complex cause-and-effect toys that require advanced thinking to understand how objects work. Objects that support toddlers' interest in cause-and-effect include elements that produce results through simple actions—knobs that twist to make a sound or to make an object move; levers that slide to open or to make a sound; latches that open or close a door or lid; nuts and bolts that screw together; and lids that screw onto or fit onto containers of various shapes and sizes. Musical instruments such as simple flutes, drums, xylophones, pianos, chimes, and bells enhance the play space with delightful sounds as children shake, tap, pluck, or blow them. Containers that fit objects only of a specific size or shape invite cause-and-effect exploration, as toddlers pursue the question, "What happens when I try this one?" Objects that encourage toddlers to notice the cause-and-effect relationships with the wind and the sun include windsocks, chimes, or sun reflectors attached to an outdoor fence. A basket of scarves or ribbons that are tied together end-to-end may engage toddlers in waving the items to explore how things move through the air. Plastic mirrors and colored, acrylic panels, stored in a basket in a sunny area of the yard, invite toddlers to explore light in playful ways.

Select toys and arrange the environment to support pretend play. Infants from one to two years of age transform ordinary objects into pretend objects that symbolize something they have experienced before. A box becomes a bed, or a block becomes a cup. A series of cardboard boxes lined up by a pair of toddlers becomes a bedroom for the two friends. Such play also reveals the children's emerging abilities to recall and reenact prior experiences in simple, pretend-play narratives. A toddler might set a table with dishes in the pretend-play area or babble in rhythmic phrases while turning the pages of a book. Support pretend play by finding out what experiences, furnishings, and clothing might be familiar to infants within their homes and families. Matching what the infants find at school with what might be commonly seen and used at home fuels pretend play for toddlers. Provide simple, toddler-size furniture and objects that the children can use as props for pretend play; clothes and accessories that toddlers can put on and take off; and duplicates of clothing that allow exploration of being the same as someone else. A variety of opportunities for children to engage in pretend play lead to increasingly complex symbolic thinking, a critically important development during the toddler years.

Offer toys that support the collection and storage of treasures. Children begin to collect items in infancy and continue this behavior throughout childhood. In the 18- to 36-month-old phase, toddlers start to collect objects for their "treasure value." They single out an object and give it special value as they hold it in their hands, store it in a pocket, or entrust it to the hands

and protection of a teacher. Toddlers often collect treasures from nature when they spend time outdoors, and they are usually interested in storing those carefully selected items in a special box or container. Support this interest by providing boxes or bins where they can safely store their treasures. Enrich toddlers' fascination with collecting special items by supplying raincoats, boots, umbrellas, hats, shoulder bags, and baskets—clothing and equipment that will allow the children to gather leaves, pinecones, flowers, and other intriguing things they may find in the play yard.

Interactions

The extent to which infants develop as confident, competent, compassionate thinkers and problem solvers is influenced by the types of play and care experiences that teachers offer. As described in other chapters, observing infants' thinking and reasoning is essential to supporting their learning. Teachers gather and note impressions of what they see and hear. From such notes and thoughts, they build curriculum by planning both indoor and outdoor learning environments that give infants opportunities to pursue their interests through play.

Infants learn throughout the day, including during moments of arrival and departure, meals, naps, and time taken for diapering, toileting, and dressing. During such caregiving routines, infants acquire increasingly complex skills related to dressing, serving food, caring for materials, and greeting and saying good-bye to people. Care experiences provide rich opportunities for infants to apply emerging skills in understanding what objects and people are like and how they work.

As infants search for information about the world around them, they often look to those who care for them as resources for learning. Infant care teachers support learning when they are available to children, being neither intrusive nor directive. Taking care to allow infants to make discoveries, they reserve for inquisitive infants the challenge of figuring out how something works or of solving a problem. When teachers take their lead from infants, watching for cues as to how and when to offer help, they build infants' confidence and competence as learners.

In addition, when teachers treat caregiving experiences as opportunities to involve infants as partners, the teachers find many ways to engage

the children in predicting what will happen next, in making decisions, and in exploring how things work. For example, when a teacher carries out a feeding routine by first holding the spoon in front of the infant's face so that the child can clearly see and anticipate what is coming next, she encourages the infant to adjust his body in preparation for receiving the spoonful of food. Doing the same with a cup, a washcloth, or any other step in a routine provides infants with many chances to make sense of how the world around them operates.

The following strategies support cognitive development.

Notice what interests each child. Observe and note what infants do in the play space and whether there are specific kinds of toys or particular actions that seem to engage their interest. Notice and name things of interest to an infant. Add to the play space objects that extend and make more complex the child's current play. This practice transforms the toy selection and play space into meaningful curriculum that is well matched to the inquisitive infant's learning. For example, when teachers observe an infant repeatedly shaking and then holding a toy still, they gather an important clue for expanding the curriculum by adding similar or somewhat more complex sound-making, cause-and-effect toys to the learning environment.

Use language to engage each child's intellect. Comment on toddlers' collecting, building, and pretend play; this provides meaningful vocabulary for toddlers to learn and use. To expand a toddler's experience, make up an impromptu song to accompany the child as he works on a task. For example, a teacher might make up a simple chant that narrates how the toddler is patting a baby doll on the back to put the doll to sleep. Offer new vocabulary to expand toddlers' experiences and increase the likelihood that toddlers will remember the experiences. For example, when toddlers put objects together, their play often involves number and quantity. Toddlers' understanding and use of vocabulary related to number and quantity (e.g., *one, two, big, small,* and *more*) will grow when teachers use those terms in narration of the children's play. In the same way, toddlers come to know the names of shapes and positions in space (e.g., *on top of, below,* or *beside*) by hearing the words used in meaningful situations. Look for opportunities to point out "how much" of an attribute an object possesses. Expressing "how long," "how high," or "how much" is another way to help children come to know terms of quantity. Likewise, telling stories is an effective way to introduce toddlers to vocabulary that relates to concepts.

Use personal care routines to support cognitive development. Once infants begin to sit up independently, mealtimes offer opportunities for the children to apply emerging skills in pouring and serving, as they can begin to use pitchers and serving spoons. Family-style meal service provides an enjoyable setting for teachers to invite infants to try their skill in pouring milk or serving a spoonful of fruit. Tables that accommodate three to six infants seated in low cube chairs make it easy for infant care teachers to sit next to the children during meals. Infants in this phase of development have already gathered much information about diapering, dressing, and napping routines. Teachers can invite infants to hold and select items, seal the tape on diapers, lift bottoms so teachers can easily slip the clean diaper underneath, reach arms into sleeves, and pick up their feet (one at a time) in order to participate—all opportunities to explore cause-and-effect, how things work, how things are alike and different, and what happens next.

Vignette

Sammy, a 20-month-old toddler, often helps out at lunchtime. He carries napkins, wipes tables, and hops up to follow his teacher, Jess, each time she leaves the table to get a spoon or a washcloth. When Jess asks him to stay seated, Sammy just gazes at her;

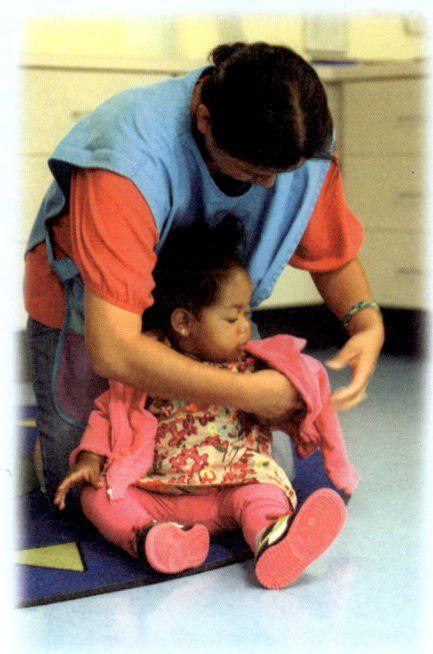 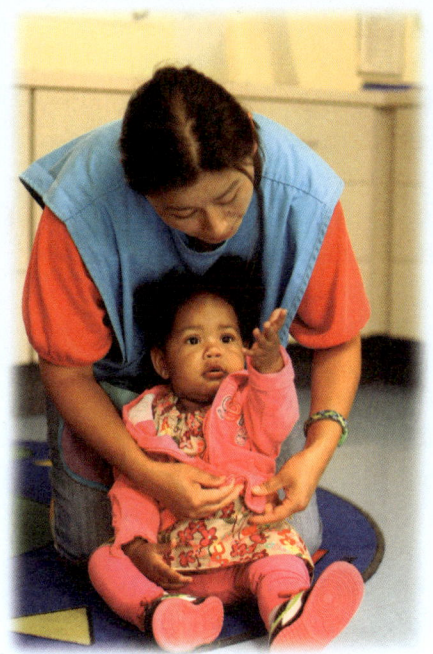

he continues to get up every time Jess does. Another teacher says to Sammy that he is Jess's little shadow. From a discussion with her master teacher, Jess got the idea to bring everything she needed with her to the table in a tub and stay seated. Jess tries out this idea and is very pleased when Sammy stays seated next to her at the table for the entire meal. She asks if he would like to help her clean up when the meal is over, and he nods.

Responsive Moment

Arnett, the master teacher, suggested to Jess that Sammy may be imitating Jess's behavior by leaving the table frequently during a meal. He is learning from Jess how to behave at the table—when she gets up, he does too. The next day, before lunch, Jess gathered in a tub all the items she thought she would need to replenish supplies and clean up messes. As Jess stayed seated for the meal, Sammy remained with her. Jess and the children at the table had a lively conversation about things they eat at home. By reflecting on her concerns in a conversation with her master teacher, Jess was able to develop a plan that, once implemented, not only helped Sammy stay at the table, but also led to spirited exchanges of ideas between Jess and the children.

Vignette

Jenna has been crawling for several weeks now and is getting quite fast at moving around. This morning, her teacher, Archie, is watching closely as Jenna crawls up the wide ramp to a platform where there are several large, plastic boxes of different sizes. Jenna crawls up to a box and sticks her head inside it, as if she were going to crawl into the box. Archie knows she will not be able to fit her entire body inside the box, but Jenna is already halfway inside it. Archie scoots up the ramp to Jenna, who may be feeling a little stuck at this point, and gently places his hand on Jenna's back, saying, "You put your head in this big box, and the rest of you is out here with me. I'm here, Jenna." Jenna pulls her head out, looks at Archie, and then vocalizes, "Ahhh, ya, ya" and gestures toward the box. Archie smiles and says, "Yes, I saw you with your head in there. I came right up here in case you needed me, but you got yourself out, didn't you?" Jenna looks back at Archie, and then at the box, a few times. Then she bangs on the box with her hands and crawls to a larger box. She glances back at Archie, who smiles, and she crawls in, fitting into the larger box quite easily. "You are in the big box, Jenna. You sure are, and I'm out here." Jenna smiles and bangs on the box while vocalizing her triumph.

Responsive Moment

Archie was already watching Jenna closely because he had seen that she was moving quickly. He knew that, in her exuberance, Jenna might not "look before leaping," so to speak. He also knew that mobile infants have an intense interest in how things move and fit in space, and they often explore with their whole bodies. While Archie knew that Jenna would not actually get stuck in the box, he thought that she might feel as if she were stuck, so he moved close to her to provide emotional and verbal support as Jenna worked out her problem. Archie acknowledged that Jenna was in a potentially frightening situation and offered comfort with a gentle touch and soothing words. Through these actions Archie conveyed his confidence in Jenna's ability to work through the situation. When Jenna pulled herself out of the box, Archie acknowledged her accomplishment. The entire episode was over in less than a minute, and Jenna moved on to conquer a larger box, seeking Archie's gaze and recognition as she did this. In response to this cue, Archie remained nearby and was available to acknowledge Jenna's efforts to learn how her body fit into the large box.

Research Highlight 1

A very young baby will imitate the actions of adults. Research by Andrew Meltzoff and colleagues has demonstrated that when infants as young as three days old see an adult stick out her tongue, they imitate the adult by sticking out their tongues in response.[10] Recent research suggests that older infants not only imitate what they see adults do, but imitate based on what they think adults intend to do. György Gergely and colleagues conducted an experiment in which they had 14-month-old infants watch an adult use his forehead to turn on a light.[11] When the infants could see that the adult turning on the light with his forehead had both of his hands occupied, the vast majority of the children used their hands, not their heads, to turn on the light, despite observing that the adult had used his head to turn on the light. This research suggests that infants do not merely reenact the behavior of adults; rather, they understand and imitate the intention underlying the behavior, which is a sophisticated social and cognitive capacity.

Research Highlight 2

The National Research Council's Committee on Early Childhood Mathematics suggests that the two domains foundational to children's math learning in early childhood are (1) number, including operations; and (2) spatial thinking, geometry, and measurement.[12] Across cultures, young infants demonstrate preverbal number knowledge and spatial understanding. For instance, five-month-olds can detect differences between sets of small numbers of objects[13] and six-month-olds demonstrate a beginning understanding of spatial relationships between objects.[14] These initial capacities are starting points for later learning of more advanced math skills.

Young children around the world use their fingers to count and show numbers. However, the specific ways in which young children use their fingers to count and show numbers vary by culture. For instance, in India some children count by using the cracks between their fingers, and in Japan, children lower and raise their fingers. In the United States and other countries, children start with the thumb and then raise the other fingers in order, using their smallest finger last. In other cultures, children start with their smallest finger and move toward the thumb. While children may use different methods to show how old they are or to count, each way works equally well.

Sample Developmental Sequences

Memory

Definition: As children develop during the first three years of life, they show awareness of past experiences and remember information about people or things. The capacity to remember allows children to differentiate between familiar and unfamiliar people and objects, anticipate and participate in parts of personal care routines, learn language, and come to know the rules of social interaction.

Beginning level: Children respond to people, things, or events. For instance, a child may turn his head toward the source of a sound or touch, or look at a toy that an adult is holding out.

Next level: Children notice people, things, and their features. For instance, they may inspect an adult's face by touching different parts, or they may stop moving to listen to noise outside.

Next level: Children recognize familiar people, objects, and routines in the environment and show awareness that familiar people still exist even when they are no longer physically present. For instance, they will look under a sofa after seeing a ball roll under it, or they may go to the window and point after mom leaves.

Next level: Children communicate one or two key details about familiar people, surroundings, things, or events that were experienced at an earlier time. For instance, they may go to get a book when seeing someone who read books with them during a previous visit, or they may greet some peers by name.

Next level: Children communicate several details about familiar people, surroundings, things, or events that were experienced at an earlier time. For instance, they can remember a series of steps in a game, or they may talk about various details of a recent family celebration, such as who was there, what the celebration was for, and what happened.

Cause-and-Effect

Definition: As children develop during the first three years of their lives, they show understanding of the connection between cause and effect. This knowledge helps them better understand the properties of objects, the patterns of human behavior, and the relationship between events and consequences. By developing an understanding of cause-and-effect, children build their ability to solve problems, make predictions, and understand the impact of their behavior on others.

Beginning level: Children respond to people, things, or events. For instance, a child may become startled by loud noises, look or turn when hearing an adult's voice from a distance, or seem surprised when a toy she is holding makes a noise.

Next level: Children repeat actions that have an effect. For example, they may shake a rattle over and over again, or they may grasp a toy, let it go, and grasp it again.

Next level: Children try out behaviors to cause things to happen. For instance, they may try to figure out how things open, such as a lid on a box, a cupboard door, or a book.

Next level: Children explore possible causes of actions, events, or behaviors. For example, they may push on different parts of a toy to make music start again, or, when hearing a beeping sound, they may look around the room to see where the sound might be coming from.

Next level: Children show understanding that actions, events, or behaviors have a specific cause. For instance, they may walk slowly while carrying a cup of milk to avoid spilling; they may play quietly, without being asked, when another child is sleeping; or they may say, "After naptime, Mommy is going to pick me up."

Engaging Families

Infant care teachers play an important role in engaging families by sharing information about and expressing enthusiasm for the cognitive development of all infants and toddlers. By encouraging families to notice the learning that takes place in the everyday experiences of very young children, teachers can help foster families' deeper understanding of infant/toddler cognitive development and strategies for supporting it.

- Suggest ideas for simple, inexpensive, homemade toys that families can use with their children to enhance cognitive development (e.g., empty toilet-paper rolls that fit into holes cut in a cardboard box give children an opportunity to explore spatial relationships).

- Point out ways in which all infants and toddlers demonstrate cognitive competencies through multiple means of expression. Encourage families to share stories from home that illustrate their children's learning.

- Suggest ways for families to incorporate the language of cognitive development into their everyday interactions with their children; for example, provide a list of words related to number sense (such as *more, same, one*) and an explanation of their developmental significance.

- Solicit family input in planning personal care routines that engage children as active participants and support the children's anticipation and understanding.

Questions for Reflection

1. How can you talk about some of the things infants and toddlers typically do—for example, request the same book or song over and over, poke each other in the face during exploration, or react strongly to changes in routine—to help families interpret them as examples of cognitive development?

2. What might be some of the similarities and differences between your (or the program's) definition of cognitive and intellectual development and that of the families in your care? How are your views reflected in your communication with families? How might you make your curriculum planning process more inclusive of diverse perspectives?

3. How does your support for children's cognitive development differ when you consider developmental level, individual development, temperament, and so

forth? For example, what does problem solving look like in a 10-month-old as compared with a 27-month-old, and how might your approach differ according to each child's abilities and needs? How do you communicate information about cognitive development to families? How do you learn from families their perspectives on development?

Concluding Thoughts

Infants and toddlers are engaged in learning with every waking moment. Their cognitive development occurs throughout the day as they explore their environment, imitate the actions of others, and interact with their teachers and each other. Their capacity to engage in exploration depends on the adults who guide and care for them. Infants and toddlers need adults to provide them with safe, appropriately challenging learning environments and play materials. They also need to establish relationships with adults that provide an emotionally secure base for exploration. These young children thrive when adults are responsive to them; responsiveness helps infants and toddlers to deepen their understanding of, among other things, cause-and-effect, sequences of actions, and the connection between concepts and words. Infants need time to solve problems. Acknowledgment from adults that communicates confidence in the infants' abilities encourages the children to try out new skills and continue to learn. To provide infants and toddlers with the types of learning environments and experiences that foster cognitive development, teachers observe the children in action and discover ways to connect with the children's learning. By approaching the active learning of infants and toddlers with a sense of wonder, teachers nurture the children's sense of wonder and their growing understanding of and fascination with the people and things in their immediate environment.

Map of the Foundations

Domain → **Cognitive Development**

Foundation → **Foundation: Attention Maintenance**

The developing ability to attend to people and things while interacting with others and exploring the environment and play materials

	8 months	18 months	36 months
Age-level description	At around eight months of age, children pay attention to different things and people in the environment in specific, distinct ways. (Bronson 2000, 64)	At around 18 months of age, children rely on order and predictability in the environment to help organize their thoughts and focus attention. (Bronson 2000, 191)	At around 36 months of age, children sometimes demonstrate the ability to pay attention to more than one thing at a time.
Examples	**For example, the child may:** • Play with one toy for a few minutes before focusing on a different toy. (6–9 mos.; Parks 2004, 12 and 26; 8 mos.; American Academy of Pediatrics 2004, 241) • Focus on a desired toy that is just out of reach while repeatedly reaching for it. (5–9 mos.; Parks 2004, 49) • Show momentary attention to board books with bright colors and simple shapes. • Attend to the play of other children. • Put toy animals into a clear container, dump them out, and then fill the container up again. (8 mos.; Meisels and others 2003, 21) • Stop moving, to focus on the infant care teacher when she starts to interact with the child.	**For example, the child may:** • Expect favorite songs to be sung the same way each time and protest if the infant care teacher changes the words. • Insist on following the same bedtime routine every night. • Nod and take the infant care teacher's hand when the teacher says, "I know you are sad because Shanti is using the book right now, and you would like a turn. Shall we go to the book basket and find another one to read together?"	**For example, the child may:** • Realize, during clean-up time, that he has put a car in the block bin and return to put it in the proper place. • Search for and find a favorite book and ask the infant care teacher to read it. • Pound the play dough with a hammer while talking with a peer.
Behaviors leading up to the foundations	**Behaviors leading up to the foundation (4 to 7 months)** During this period, the child may: • Remain calm and focused on people, interesting toys, or interesting sounds for a minute or so. (1–6 mos.; Parks 2004, 9) • Explore a toy by banging, mouthing, or looking at it. (Scaled score of 9 for 3:26–4:05 mos.; Bayley 2006, 52)	**Behaviors leading up to the foundation (9 to 17 months)** During this period, the child may: • Pay attention to the infant care teacher's voice without being distracted by other noises in the room. (9–11 mos.; Parks 2004; 12) • Focus on one toy or activity for a while when really interested. (By 12 mos.; American Academy of Pediatrics 2004, 241)	**Behaviors leading up to the foundation (19 to 35 months)** During this period, the child may: • Play alone with toys for several minutes at a time before moving on to different activity. (18–24 mos.; Parks 2004, 15) • Sit in a parent's lap to read a book together. (Scaled score of 10 for 21:16–22:15 mos.; Bayley 2006)

Teacher Resources

Begley, S. "Your Child's Brain." *Newsweek* 127, no. 8 (February 19, 1996): 55–61.

Burchinal, M. R., and others. "Quality of Center Child Care and Infant Cognitive and Language Development." *Child Development* 67, no. 2 (April 1996): 606–20.

Families and Work Institute. *Brain Development in Young Children: New Frontiers for Research, Policy and Practice* (conference report). New York: Families and Work Institute, 1996.

Galinsky, E. 2010. *Mind in the Making: The Seven Essential Life Skills Every Child Needs.* New York: HarperCollins Publishers, 2010.

Gandini, L. "Teachers and Children Together: Constructing New Learning." *Childcare Information Exchange* 108 (March/April 1996): 43–46.

Gopnik, A. "How Babies Think." *Scientific American* 303, no. 1 (July 2010): 76–81.

Gopnik, A., A. Meltzoff, and P. Kuhl. *The Scientist in the Crib: Minds, Brains, and How Children Learn.* New York: William Morrow, 1999.

Hawley, T. "Starting Smart: How Early Experiences Affect Brain Development. An Ounce of Prevention Fund Paper." Chicago: Ounce of Prevention Fund, 1998.

Hirsh-Pasek, K., R. Golinkoff, and D. Eyer. *Einstein Never Used Flash Cards: How Our Children Really Learn—and Why They Need to Play More and Memorize Less.* Emmaus, PA: Rodale Press, 2004.

Lally, J. R. "Brain Research, Infant Learning, and Child Care Curriculum." *Child Care Information Exchange* 121 (May/June 1998): 46–48.

Lally, J. R., Y. L. Torres, and P. C. Phelps. "Caring for Infants and Toddlers in Groups: Necessary Considerations for Emotional, Social, and Cognitive Development." *Zero to Three* 14, no. 5 (April/May 1994): 1–37.

National Research Council and Institute of Medicine. *From Neurons to Neighborhoods: The Science of Early Childhood Development.* Edited by J. P. Shonkoff and D. A. Phillips, Committee on Integrating the Science of Early Childhood Development. Washington, DC: National Academies Press, 2000.

Perry, B. D., and others. "Childhood Trauma, the Neurobiology of Adaptation, and 'Use-dependent' Development of the Brain: How 'States' Become 'Traits'." *Infant Mental Health Journal* 16, no. 4 (Winter 1995): 271–91.

Pratt, M. "The Importance of Infant/Toddler Interactions." *Young Children* 54, no. 4 (July 1999) 26–29.

Restak, R. M. *The Infant Mind.* Garden City, NY: Doubleday and Company, Inc., 1986.

Shaffer, L. "Using Our Experiences With Infants to Tell the Stories of Their Capabilities." *Child Care Information Exchange* 31 (January/February 2009): 30–33.

Shore, R. M. *Rethinking the Brain—New Insights into Early Development.* New York: Families and Work Institute, 1997.

Wadsworth, B. *Piaget's Theory of Cognitive Development: An Introduction for Students of Psychology and Education.* New York: David McKay Company, 1973.

Endnotes

1. A. Gopnik, *The Philosophical Baby: What Children's Minds Tell Us About Truth, Love, and the Meaning of Life* (New York: Farrar, Straus and Giroux, 2009), p. 5.

2. K. L. Madole and L. M. Oakes, "Making Sense of Infant Categorization: Stable Processes and Changing Representations," *Developmental Review* 19, no. 2 (1999): 263.

3. R. J. Sternberg and E. L. Grigorenko, "Why We Need to Explore Development in Its Cultural Context," *Merrill-Palmer Quarterly* 50, no. 3 (July 2004): 369–86.

4. B. Rogoff and P. Chavajay, "What's Become of Research on the Cultural Basis of Cognitive Development?," *American Psychologist* 50, no. 10 (1995): 859–77.

5. R. J. Sternberg and E. L. Grigorenko, "Why We Need to Explore Development in Its Cultural Context," *Merrill-Palmer Quarterly* 50, no. 3 (July 2004): 369–86.

6. National Research Council and Institute of Medicine, *From Neurons to Neighborhoods: The Science of Early Childhood Development* (Washington, DC: National Academies Press, 2000), pp. 146–149.

7. G. J. Whitehurst and C. J. Lonigan, "Child Development and Emergent Literacy," *Child Development* 69, no. 3 (June 1998): 848–72.

8. E. Kálló and G. Balog, *The Origins of Free Play* (Budapest, Hungary: Pikler-Lóczy Társaság, 2005), p. 14.

9. National Research Council and Institute of Medicine, *From Neurons to Neighborhoods: The Science of Early Childhood Development* (Washington, DC: National Academies Press, 2000), p. 148.

10. A. N. Meltzoff and M. K. Moore, "Imitation, Memory, and the Representation of Persons," *Infant Behavior and Development* 17 (1994): 83–99.

11. G. Gergely, H. Bekkering, and I. Király, "Rational Imitation in Preverbal Infants: Babies May Opt for a Simpler Way to Turn on a Light After Watching an Adult Do It," *Nature* 415 (February 2002): 755–56.

12. National Research Council, *Mathematics Learning in Early Childhood: Paths Toward Excellence and Equity* (Washington, DC: National Academies Press, 2009), p. 2.

13. M. M. Haith and J. B. Benson, "Infant Cognition" (New York: John Wiley and Sons, Inc., 1998), p. 225.

14. P.C. Quinn and others, "Development of an Abstract Category Representation for the Spatial Relation 'Between' in 6-to-10 Month Old Infants," *Developmental Psychology* 39, no. 1 (January 2003): 151–63.

Bibliography

Gergely, G., H. Bekkering, and I. Király. "Rational Imitation in Preverbal Infants: Babies May Opt for a Simpler Way to Turn on a Light After Watching an Adult Do It." *Nature* 415 (February 2002): 755–56.

Gopnik, A. *The Philosophical Baby: What Children's Minds Tell Us About Truth, Love, and the Meaning of Life.* New York: Farrar, Straus and Giroux, 2009.

Haith, M. M., and J. B. Benson. "Infant Cognition," in *Handbook of Child Psychology Vol. 2: Cognition, Perception, and Language.* 5th ed. Edited by D. Kuhn and R. Siegler. Editor-in-Chief William Damon. New York: John Wiley and Sons, Inc., 1998.

Kálló, E., and G. Balog. *The Origins of Free Play.* Budapest, Hungary: Pikler-Lóczy Társaság, 2005.

Madole, K. L., and L. M. Oakes. "Making Sense of Infant Categorization: Stable Processes and Changing Representations." *Developmental Review* 19, no. 2 (1999): 263–96.

Meltzoff, A. N., and M. K. Moore. "Imitation, Memory, and the Representation of Persons." *Infant Behavior and Development* 17 (1994): 83–99.

National Research Council. *Mathematics Learning in Early Childhood: Paths Toward Excellence and Equity.* Edited by C. T. Cross, T. A. Woods, and H. Schweingruber, Committee on Early Childhood Mathematics. Center for Education, Division of Behavioral and Social Sciences and Education. Washington, DC: National Academies Press, 2009.

National Research Council and Institute of Medicine. *From Neurons to Neighborhoods: The Science of Early Childhood Development.* Edited by J. P. Shonkoff and D. A. Phillips, Committee on Integrating the Science of Early Childhood Development. Washington, DC: National Academies Press, 2000.

Quinn, P.C., and others. "Development of an Abstract Category Representation for the Spatial Relation 'Between' in 6-to-10 Month Old Infants." *Developmental Psychology* 39, no. 1 (January 2003): 151–63.

Rogoff, B., and P. Chavajay. "What's Become of Research on the Cultural Basis of Cognitive Development?," *American Psychologist* 50, no. 10 (1995): 859–77.

Sternberg, R. J., and E. L. Grigorenko. "Why We Need to Explore Development in Its Cultural Context." *Merrill-Palmer Quarterly* 50, no. 3 (July 2004): 369–86.

Whitehurst, G. J., and C. J. Lonigan. "Child Development and Emergent Literacy." *Child Development* 69, no. 3 (June 1998): 848–72.

Chapter 6
Perceptual and Motor Development

Perception refers to the process of taking in, organizing, and interpreting sensory information. Perception is multimodal, with multiple sensory inputs contributing to motor responses.[1] When an infant turns her head in response to the visual and auditory cues of the sight of a face and the sound of a voice, she exhibits this type of perception. Researchers Lorraine Bahrick, Robert Lickliter, and Ross Flom consider intersensory redundancy—the fact that the senses provide overlapping information—a "cornerstone of perceptual development."[2]

Motor development unfolds with perceptual development; it refers to changes in a child's ability to control his body movements, from the infant's first spontaneous waving and kicking movements to the adaptive control of reaching, locomotion, and complex sport skills.[3] The term *motor behavior* describes all movements of the body, including movements of the eyes (as in the gaze) and the infant's developing control of the head. Gross motor actions include the movement of large limbs or the whole body, such as walking. Fine motor behaviors include the use of fingers to grasp and manipulate objects. Motor behaviors such as touching and grasping are forms of exploratory activity.[4]

As infants develop increasing motor competence, they use perceptual information when choosing which motor actions to take.[5] For example, they may adjust their crawling or walking in response to the degree to which surfaces are rigid, slippery, or slanted.[6] Motor movements, includ-

ing movements of the eyes, arms, legs, and hands, provide most of the perceptual information that infants receive.[7] Young children's bodies undergo remarkable changes in the early childhood years. In describing this development, Adolph and Avolio state, "Newborns are extremely top-heavy with large heads and torsos and short, weak legs. As infants grow, their body fat and muscle mass are redistributed. In contrast to newborns, toddlers' bodies have a more cylindrical shape, and they have a larger ratio of muscle mass to body fat, especially in the legs."[8] These changes in weight, size, percentage of body fat, and muscle strength provide perceptual and motor challenges to infants as they practice a variety of actions.[9] This dramatic physical development occurs within the broad context of overall development. As infants master challenges, their perceptual and motor behavior reflects their interpersonal orientation and social environment.

The extent and variety of infant perceptual and motor behavior are remarkable. Infants and toddlers spend a significant part of their days engaged in motor behavior of one type or another. By three-and-a-half months of age, infants have made between three and six million eye movements during their waking hours.[10] Infants who crawl and walk have been found to spend roughly half of their waking hours involved in motor behavior, approximately five to six hours per day.[11] On a daily basis, infants who are walking "take more than 9,000 steps and travel the distance of more than 29 football fields. They travel over nearly a dozen different indoor and outdoor surfaces varying in friction, rigidity and texture. They visit nearly every room in their homes and they engage in balance and locomotion in the context of varied activities."[12]

Early research in motor development involved detailed observational studies that documented the progression of infant motor skills and presented an understanding of infant motor behavior as a sequence of universal, biologically programmed steps.[13, 14, 15, 16] More recent research in motor development tends to emphasize action in the context of behavior and development in the perceptual, cognitive, and social domains.[17] In particular, contemporary accounts of infant motor development address the strong relationship between perception and action.[18, 19, 20] This research also focuses on the relationship between actions and the environment, and on the importance of motives in motor behavior, especially social and explorative motives.[21, 22, 23] Although historical approaches may encourage professionals to focus on the relationship between growing perceptual and motor skills and the child's increasingly sophisticated manipulation and understanding of objects, contemporary understanding suggests the value of observing this progression over time. The ways in which these developing behaviors and abilities play a role in the social and emotional aspects of the child's life and functioning, such as forming early relationships and building an understanding of others, may be noteworthy.

The contemporary view suggests that thinking about perceptual and motor development can be inclusive of infants and toddlers with disabilities or other special needs. Like children who are typically developing, children who have disabilities that affect their

perceptual or motor development want to explore and interact with the people and things in their immediate environment. Although the perceptual and motor development of children with disabilities or other special needs may differ from typical development, sensitive and responsive caregivers can provide alternative ways to engage children's drive to explore, building on each child's interests and strengths and supporting his or her overall physical and psychological health.

Pioneering researchers in infant motor development used novel and painstaking methods to study the progression of infant skill acquisition.[24, 25] Their findings were presented for both professionals and the public in the form of milestone charts that depicted motor skill acquisition as a clear progression through a series of predictable stages related to chronological age.[26, 27] More recent research in the area of perceptual and motor development has indicated substantial variability between children in the pathways to acquiring noteworthy motor milestones, such as sitting and walking.[28, 29] Each child may take a unique developmental pathway toward attainment of important motor milestones.[30] Crawling, for example, is not a universal stage. Research clearly shows that some children do not crawl before they walk.[31] Although most children walk independently at around age one, the normal range for acquisition of this behavior in Western cultures is very broad, between nine and 17 months of age.[32] Traditionally, age has been treated as the primary predictor of when landmark motor behaviors occur, but studies now indicate that experience may be a stronger predictor of the emergence of both crawling and walking.[33, 34]

It is important to recognize that, though developmental charts may show motor development unfolding in the form of a smooth upward progression toward mastery, the development of individual children often does not follow a smooth upward trajectory. In fact, "detours" and steps backward are common as development unfolds.[35] Infant motor development can be understood as a process in which change occurs as the infant actively adapts to varying circumstances and new tasks.[36] Thelen demonstrated this experimentally in her well-known study in which three-month-old babies, still too young to coordinate their movements to sit, reach, or crawl, learned to coordinate their kicks in order to engage in the novel task of making a mobile move.[37] Cultural and historical factors, including caregivers' behavior, also affect the ways in which infants engage in motor behaviors. For example, Adolph and Berger observed that mothers in Jamaica and Mali "train" infants to sit by propping up three- to four-month-old infants with pillows in a special hole in the ground designed to provide back support.[38]

For years, researchers, educators, and early childhood professionals have emphasized the interrelatedness of the developmental domains. The current research supports an even greater appreciation of the profound role of interrelatedness and interdependence of factors, domains, and processes in development.[39] The developmental domains are linked not only with one another, but also with factors such as culture, social relationships, experi-

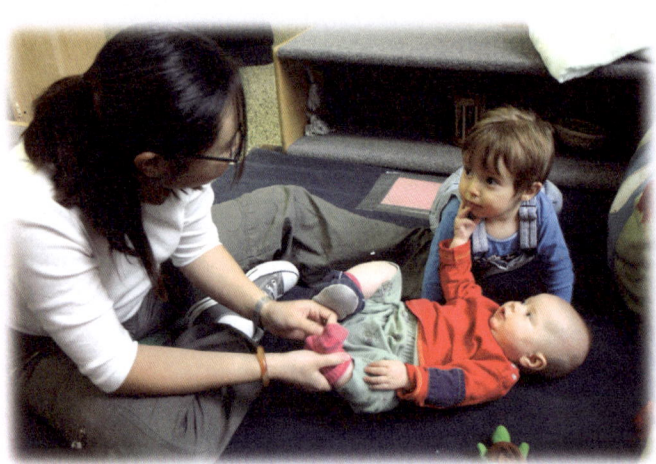

ence, physical health, mental health, and brain functioning.[40] In the case of perceptual and motor behavior, Diamond has observed that perception, motor behavior, and cognition occur in the context of culture, emotion, social relationships, and experience, which in turn influence physical and mental health as well as overall brain functioning.[41] Bertenthal has proposed that perception and motor action are interrelated rather than autonomous processes.[42] They may be best viewed as different components of an action system. Common behaviors such as reaching and turning the head for visual tracking illustrate the interrelatedness of the motor, perceptual, cognitive, and social–emotional domains in infant development. Even as very young infants, children are highly motivated to explore, gain information, observe, and engage their physical and social environments.[43] As Gibson explains, "We don't simply see, we look."[44] Research by Berthier indicates that "infant reaching is not simply a neural program that is triggered by the presence of a goal object, but that infants match the kinematics of their reaches to the task and their goals."[45]

Perception and motor action play a key role in children's experiences and psychological processes.[46] They also contribute to human psychological development in general, as "behavior is movement"[47] and psychology can be defined as the study of human behavior. It has been proposed that infants' use of social information to guide their motor behavior in physically challenging or unfamiliar situations provides an excellent means to study infant social cognition.[48]

Of the four major developmental domains, perceptual and motor development may appear to unfold independently of the other domains. However, as recent research on perceptual and motor development suggests, development in every domain is related to children's perceptual and motor abilities. Even the social–emotional domain comes into play when children engage in motor behavior in physically challenging or unfamiliar situations. When planning curriculum for infants and toddlers in the perceptual and motor development domain, teachers need to focus on ways to support children's processing of sensory information and fine and gross motor movements. Yet, to be effective, the planning should occur in a broad context in which each child's overall development is observed, documented, and considered.

Guiding Principles

Recognize the child's developing abilities

Even the youngest infant has perceptual and motor skills. When observing a young infant exploring and experimenting with movements and postural changes, teachers witness an extraordinary developmental process. The infant's innate drive to move and gain control over body movements is in action all the time. Part of developing a relationship with an infant is to communicate recognition of the child's active, self-motivated role in perceptual and motor development. For instance, a teacher may comment to a young infant, "I see you kicking and kicking your legs," or "I know you are busy balancing on your side right now. I need to pick you up. We are going outside where you can practice some more." As infants become increasingly mobile, begin to walk and even run, and eventually coordinate movements such as walking on a low balance beam or holding a writing tool, adults can continually share the children's sense of accomplishment with them and validate their motivation to take on physical challenges. When caring for a child with a disability or other special need that affects perception or movement, teachers benefit from communicating with family members and specialists who work with the child, learning about the focus of the child's perceptual and motor development. This information helps teachers to anticipate, recognize, and support the child's emerging perceptual and motor abilities.

Encourage self-directed movement

In a space with equipment that supports self-directed movement, infants and toddlers freely express their natural urge to move. Children move freely in space that is safe. They need equipment that is stable, an appropriate height, and appropriately challenging. The use of developmental barriers allows teachers to provide equipment for children who may be ready to explore with such equipment, while protecting other children who are not. Furnishings and equipment for

routine care can also support movement—for example, a diapering surface with stairs for toddlers to climb up, or one surrounded by sturdy railings that allow mobile infants to pull up to a standing position safely. Equipment that children can use without assistance (e.g., small stools or chairs) supports their movement as well. Teachers also encourage children's self-directed movement by expressing appreciation and giving children the opportunity to initiate action. For instance, rather than lifting a child and putting him in a small chair, a teacher may wait while the child gets into it on his own. Or rather than putting a toy in a baby's hand, a teacher may sit quietly while the infant balances carefully on his or her side and reaches for a toy. Encouraging free movement and respecting the child's initiative go hand in hand.

Respect individual differences

Infants and toddlers differ from one another in the way they explore movement and in the timing of different developmental milestones. One infant may begin walking at nine months, and another at 16 months. Some infants are often content to stay relatively still and observe what is going on around them, while others often have an intense urge to move their bodies. One child may practice a skill over and over again, such as pulling up and then squatting down, and another may transition quickly from cruising to walking. The speed at which children master skills, and the learning strategies they use, differ greatly. For example, one child may be content to let go and fall back to the floor, while another carefully lowers herself to kneeling. Differences in fine motor development are just as pronounced. For example, one infant may show readiness to feed himself with utensils at nine months, and another child of the same age may prefer to be fed by an adult. Infants and toddlers may develop rapidly in some areas and slowly in others. An infant who uses a fork or spoon at nine months may not walk until 16 months of age. Differences among children are influenced by both experience and unique personal traits. Learning about individual differences and preparing an environment and routines that adaptively support individual children is important and often rewarding. Teachers have to keep in mind that a child who is developing atypically has traits and learning strategies that are unrelated to his or her disability or special needs. It is essential for teachers to get to know every child well and adapt accordingly, both in the way they interact with each child and by setting up an appropriately challenging environment.

Provide a safe place for each age group

It is challenging to provide care in a setting when the children's ages range from a few months to 36 months. The space, materials, and equipment must meet the needs of active, self-motivated learners who are at vastly different levels of development. Young infants need floor space that is warm, firm, clean, and safe so they can kick, roll, and balance. A space that is kept free of traffic by a developmental barrier prevents young infants from being stepped on or bumped into by older children. Mobile infants often want to explore and move from place to place during most of their waking hours.

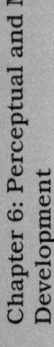

They thrive in open space, with shelves and other sturdy objects to pull up on and a completely safe environment that allows them to explore freely. As infants become increasingly mobile, they often carry items with them as they move. Toddlers move bigger, heavier things as they move through space. In general, toddlers need plenty of opportunities for large motor exploration. They often like to help move tables and chairs and bring toys outside. Additionally, toddlers frequently stand rather than sit when they work at shelves and tables. Teachers can support self-directed movement of each age group by paying close attention to the children's interests and needs and by providing time and materials appropriate for active exploration.

Be available to children as they move and explore

As infants and toddlers explore objects, climb, or play with each other, they need a familiar, caring adult nearby. Because perceptual and motor development occurs without any instruction, teachers may sometimes feel that all they have to do is prepare the environment. Yet the teacher's essential role in supporting this development includes much more than arranging the space, equipment, and materials in the child care setting. The teacher's attentive presence and emotional and physical availability allow children to move away and explore and, when they feel the urge, to return to the teacher. A child may check in by simply looking back or calling to the teacher with words or a vocalization that communicates, "Look at me!" Another child may climb into the teacher's lap and rest and watch others for a while. Teachers also need to be present to intervene in potential conflicts, such as when one child is going up a ramp or slide and another is coming down or when two children want the same object. A teacher who is available, observes, and intervenes when necessary provides the emotional nurturance infants and toddlers need to move and explore to their hearts' delight.

Summary of the Foundations

The perceptual and motor development domain consists of three foundations:

1. Perceptual Development
2. Gross Motor Development
3. Fine Motor Development

Please refer to the map of the perceptual and motor development foundations on page 141 for a visual explanation of the terminology used in the infant/toddler learning and development foundations.

Environments and Materials

Teachers are the architects of the infant's environment. After the environment is designed, teachers continually scan areas and make judgments about what is safe but challenging for children's emerging skills. Toddlers usually repeat over and over again whatever skill they are perfecting. For instance, they may be working on walking up and down a small incline while keeping their balance. When the challenge diminishes, it may be time to introduce a steeper incline such as a small grassy mound, or the children may discover for themselves different challenges in the environment. The following strategies support perceptual and motor development.

Choose materials that support perceptual and motor development, focusing on the children's interests and how to expand on those interests. A child may seem fascinated with using tools to shape play dough. Offer different shapes that toddlers can use to mold the dough. Children may sense the contours of the different shapes, which may lead to interesting discoveries. Place on the floor or on a low table items that toddlers can use for hand and finger activities—for example, simple puzzles with knobs, peg and board sets, and large beads that can be placed on a string.

Make sure there are plenty of opportunities for movement and large motor play, both indoors and outdoors. Toddlers are active movers who are still perfecting their basic movement skills. Running and jumping can be consuming interests. Provide riding toys for toddlers, but be sure to manage traffic patterns when children use this equipment. Avoid exercise saucers or walkers, as they restrict movement and may not be permitted by licensing regulations. Although most infants seem to enjoy being upright, devices such as walkers and exercise saucers can place undue stress on immature body areas.

Provide safe but challenging spaces where children can move, both indoors and outdoors. Infants who are not yet walking need safe yet challenging spaces protected from foot traffic of older children and adults; a clean floor free of small objects to mouth (and perhaps swallow); different levels to explore, such as a small ramp or a few steps; soft areas where they can sit and rest; and reachable, interesting objects to explore. Crawling babies need plenty of room to move. As babies become increasingly adept at crawling, different surfaces, such as a slightly high mat or big pillows placed on the floor to crawl over, make moving more challenging. Toys should be available on low, accessible shelves that are labeled with pictures of the toys; this makes it easy for both the child and the teacher to put away the toys.

Consider the arrangement of furniture and space in establishing physical boundaries for moving and exploring. Strategically placed shelves and large furniture can define and limit areas of play and rest as well as areas for foot traffic.

Consider the young infant's need for sheltered spaces. Place cribs or bassinets in a quiet, protected area where babies can sleep undisturbed, yet still be observed at all times. When not asleep in a crib or bassinet, the young infant needs a firm but comfortable surface upon which she can lie, protected from the movement of older children. She also needs to be shielded from bright lights and loud noises. While outside, infants can lie in carriages or on a soft blanket on the ground in a shady, sheltered spot.

Consider safety in arranging the environment. Infants need a safe, roomy area in which they can move as they learn to roll and push up. Place shatterproof mirrors in places where infants can see their movements. Sometimes infants become quite interested in seeing themselves move their bodies. Scan the room for safety, as infants' emerging fine motor abilities allow them to use their fingers to pick up and mouth small objects and poke fingers into interesting places. Set up

mats or carpeted areas that offer padding for crawling infants. Mirrors and pictures, especially of the children and their families hung at a level for easy viewing, add familiarity and interest to the environment.

Consider the child's ease of movement in setting up the physical environment. Low chairs and tables where toddlers can eat or work on simple art projects or puzzles allow ease of movement.

Offer variety in sensory and motor experiences and materials. When providing sensory materials such as water or sand, consider the variety of props you put out and the different skills that can be practiced with the various items. For instance, if there is water play in individual pans, small sponge blocks float and can be squeezed. On another day, children may become interested in scooping and pouring various materials. Offer different challenges for large motor play—for example, low climbers, rocking horses, large boxes to climb into and out of, tunnels to crawl through, and low slides.

Use everyday objects and materials to offer opportunities for perceptual and motor experiences. Boxes with lids that can be opened and closed are interesting to explore and allow little fingers to practice those motions. Filling, carrying, and dumping are favorite activities of toddlers. Shopping bags to fill with wads of paper or small toys, large empty water bottles that can be filled with clothespins or other small objects, and baskets (with handles) that can be filled with precious objects are just a few examples of items that support manipulative and moving abilities. Additionally, soft scarves placed within reach of young infants give the babies opportunities to explore through fingering or grasping, and cardboard books with bite-able, easy-to-turn pages are usually appealing for older babies and young toddlers to explore and manipulate.

Interactions

A primary principle in fostering physical development is respecting that babies are not taught movement. They achieve a specific competency when they are ready for that specific challenge. Gonzales-Mena and Eyer state: "Don't put babies into positions they cannot get into by themselves. The process of *getting into* a position is more important than *being in* the position—the process promotes development."[49] To support physical development, it is important to gather information from the child's family about how the infant is cared for at home. This information will help guide how to interact with the child and how to carry out care routines such as feeding, sleeping, and toileting. It is noteworthy that all routines offer opportunities for infants to acquire body skills.

The following strategies support perceptual and motor development.

Provide the infant with freedom to move. When infants are awake, they need freedom to move. Place a young infant on his back on a flat surface, which will allow him to stretch out and wave his arms and cycle his legs. He may catch sight of his hands and be fascinated. Describe to the baby what he sees; for instance, you might say, "Oh, look at your hands and fingers!" or "See how your legs move up and down?" This practice communicates to the baby that you are interested in his actions. Avoid restrictive equipment such as swings and bouncers, as they severely limit a baby's possibilities for moving.

See things from the infant's perspective. Appreciate the perceptual and motor experiences of a young infant who can move by rolling; this can be done by getting down on the floor at the infant's eye level and seeing the child's perspective. Crawl with babies who are beginning to crawl. They often enjoy having an adult follow behind them as they move about. Place objects within the babies' reach when they are sitting, as infants enjoy reaching for things. Suitable objects include small, easy-to-grasp manipulatives such as musical shakers, large plastic beads to pull apart, and soft dolls to mouth, feel, and squeeze. Having a few toys near a baby who is lying down or sitting will draw the attention of the child without overwhelming her. Likewise, a mirror or a colorful toy located within a young infant's range of sight can provide interesting possibilities for learning. Place these objects in ways that encourage babies to turn and reach while they are sitting; this will help them to practice balancing the head and upper body. During the early stages of development some infants will gain the ability to roll to the side or flip over, onto the stomach, holding their heads up and looking around. When holding young infants, use different positions or alternate right and left sides while supporting their heads. This practice gives babies different perspectives and allows them to use and strengthen different muscle groups. Additionally, take infants to interesting places or change what they see by placing them in different locations—look out the window with them, go outside, or move them to another room. This changes their view and offers them a variety of sensations, such as seeing leaves move with the wind or feeling a breeze on one's cheeks.

Help build the infant's feelings of comfort, security, and awareness of his body. Feed an infant when he seems hungry and put him down to rest when he appears to need sleep. Being responsive in this way helps a baby become aware of his body's messages. Most infants begin to develop their own patterns of hunger and need for sleep. Hold a baby while bottle-feeding. This practice adds the special comfort of touch to the experience. Describe what is happening during diapering and ask the infant to participate. This communication conveys respect for her body and connects words with areas of her body that she can feel as they are being moved and touched. A comment such as, "Oh, you climbed up two steps" acknowledges an infant's accomplishment and gives the message that an adult shares in the child's pride of accomplishment. Help new walkers accept that falls are part of the learning process, and thereby encourage infants to keep learning by taking on physical challenges. Magda Gerber suggests that the teacher's role is to be attentive and available and to appreciate and enjoy what the baby does.[50]

Use common routines, activities, and behaviors to allow for practice of perceptual and motor skills.

- Let eating become a shared project. Have one spoon for the baby and one for the teacher, and trade spoons during the meal. While feeding, infants often touch or mash food as they explore texture and consistency. It is also common for an infant to reach for a spoon the teacher is using to feed her. Provide finger foods—foods a baby can pick up—to allow infants to perfect their pincer grasp, which usually appears at around 10 months of age. Allow a baby who is developing the ability to grasp things begin, if he wants, to hold his own bottle of formula or breast milk. Offer foods that can be picked up with the fingers or easily spooned, and a cup that is easy to grasp and support. Eating time provides great opportunities for infants to work on hand–eye coordination as well as to gain an overall sense of competence. Draw attention to the children's sensory experiences by talking with infants at mealtime; for example, comment on how the food tastes or on the noise the food makes as it is chewed and crunched by an infant.

- Look at cardboard books with infants and talk about the books while the infants handle them. Give infants the chance to use their fingers to turn pages and point to whatever attracts their attention.

- Offer a little help to toddlers who, as they are mastering the use and coordination of fingers, may occasionally show signs of frustration. For example, moving the mouth of a container closer to a toddler's hand may be all that is needed for the child to put a bead into a jar.

- Sing songs that have different hand motions—such as "Wheels on the Bus" or "Twinkle, Twinkle"—and go slowly to allow infants to try to control, time, and coordinate movements. For example, when an infant begins clapping two hands together, she is learning to coordinate the two sides of her body. Infants may also enjoy games that encourage the development of fine motor skills.

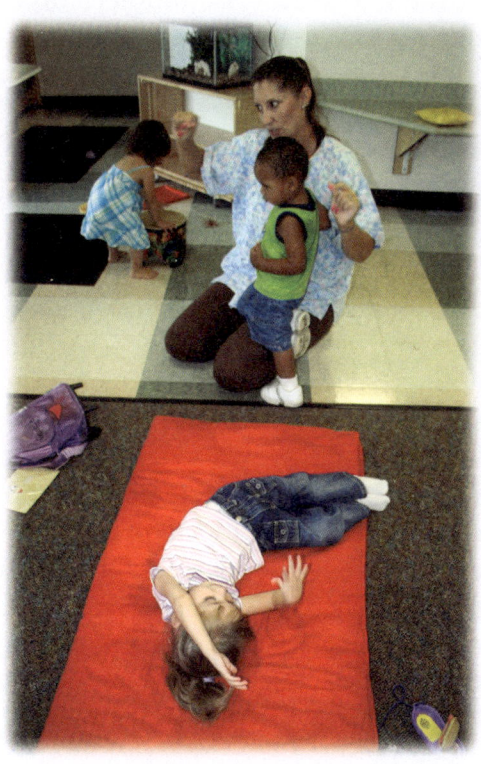

One example is This Little Piggy Went to Market.

- To foster movement among infants and toddlers, establish specific times for playing music. This practice builds expectation in the children, and they can begin to look forward to the activity. Older toddlers enjoy when a teacher initiates music games such as "Hokey Pokey" or "Ring Around the Rosie."
- Create times for reading one-on-one with toddlers. They may enjoy following a simple story line, turning page after page. Sometimes a small group of toddlers may spontaneously gather as a teacher reads to one or two children, and each child may want a chance to turn a page.

Acknowledge each child's accomplishments. Comment on infants' efforts and enjoy their accomplishments with them. A comment such as "You made it to the top of the ladder!" builds a child's confidence, which grows with each new feat.

Vignette

Seven-month-old Abasi is seated comfortably in teacher Stephen's lap, ready for lunch. Abasi tugs at his bib and watches intently as Stephen fills a bowl with orange baby food. Abasi opens his mouth when Stephen holds up a full spoon for him to see. Stephen gently moves the spoon to Abasi's lips, and Abasi closes his mouth on the spoon. Almost immediately, Abasi spits out the spoon and food and grimaces. Stephen is surprised. Abasi refuses another bite and ends up having a bottle instead. Stephen mentions this episode to Abasi's grandmother at pickup time. She laughs and says, "His favorite food is peaches, but that was carrots. I told his Mama that it would be a nasty surprise for him!" Abasi watches as the two adults laugh together. Stephen comments, "Abasi, you looked at the orange color and expected your favorite—peaches. What a surprise to taste carrots!"

Responsive Moment

Stephen recognizes that Abasi had expected peaches based on the color of the food on the spoon. Stephen documents this observation as evidence of Abasi's perceptual development. Abasi's grandmother anticipated Abasi's reaction to carrots, and she and Stephen share a moment of understanding. Stephen plans to let Abasi have a tiny taste of each food from now on, and he will tell Abasi ahead of time about the types of food that are prepared for him.

Vignette

Leon is five months old. He is the youngest child in Mona and Brandy's Early Head Start classroom. The classroom can get very busy, as four of the eight children are active toddlers, and babies on the floor need to be protected from bigger bodies and toys. Last week, Mona and Brandy rearranged some furniture and barriers to create a space where Leon can safely move his body on the floor. Brandy is Leon's primary care teacher. She observes Leon moving in the protected space they set up for him. Leon kicks up both of his legs, reaches up with his arms, and rolls onto his side. As he makes these movements, he vocalizes, "Aaauuuuu, aaaauuuuuu." Leon then rolls back onto his back and repeats the action a few times. He grabs his right toes with his right hand, and he stays on his side a few seconds longer before rolling onto his back again. Occasionally, Leon kicks vigorously, pumping his arms and legs, and then he begins to roll his body again. Brandy quickly makes a note about how Leon is grabbing his toes while on his side, as she has not seen this behavior previously.

Leon's loud vocalizations draw the attention of two toddlers who have been playing in the book corner. As they approach Leon, Brandy also moves toward him. The children ask if they can hold the baby. Brandy smiles and says, "Let's watch him for a while. He is learning how to move his body. Isn't that right, Leon?" Leon continues his movements without acknowledging his observers. After watching Leon for a few moments Brandy says to the toddlers, "When Leon shows interest in being held, you can sit with us then. I'll come find you." The toddlers nod to each other and return to the book corner.

Responsive Moment

Brandy sees that Leon is moving his body more and more. Leon's mother says that at home he is happy to roll around on a blanket by himself for a little while. Brandy consulted with her teaching partner, and they decided to rearrange the classroom to create a space where Leon can safely move on the floor. Brandy makes sure that she can easily see Leon in his protected space and that she is able to enter the space quickly when Leon needs her or when she has a spare moment to sit with him.

Brandy is also aware that the toddlers can enter Leon's protected space quite easily even though Leon cannot leave the space without help. Brandy keeps a close eye on the children who approach the barrier. She makes a point of helping the toddlers recognize Leon's activity while also supporting their interest in being with him.

Research Highlight 1

"Development can be a process of moving one step backward for every two steps forward."[51] After an infant masters the act of crawling, she eventually stops focusing on her proficiency in that skill to take on the new challenge of walking. Although the infant will gain a more efficient form of locomotion by learning to walk, it will take her a while to achieve the level of proficiency in walking that she has already achieved in crawling. Infants who are new to walking may revert to crawling when trying

to get somewhere quickly. Yet despite making this adjustment to move more quickly, infants seem to prefer to face new obstacles in their newly learned upright posture rather than in their crawling position.[52] Some researchers suggest that when first learning to walk, infants may be motivated to give up crawling for the novelty of walking even though it involves a sacrifice of proficiency in movement.

Research Highlight 2

A large body of research suggests that infants between the ages of about five months and seven months begin to use visual information from their environment to help guide the motor actions they take. Infants will adjust their reach or grasp according to visual and other sensory cues from the environment. Building upon these findings in a recent study, Claxton and colleagues suggest that infants use perceptual information not only to guide their actions in the moment, but also to plan what they will do with an object in the immediate future.[53] In this study, infants who were ten and a half months old adjusted how they reached for an object based upon what they were planning to do with the object. For instance, when the infants intended to throw a ball, they reached toward the ball more quickly than if they planned to fit the ball into a tube.[54] This research suggests that early in life, infants use perceptual cues in sophisticated ways to guide their behavior.

Developmental Sequence

Fine Motor

Definition: Through touching, grasping, and manual manipulation, children learn about the features of people, objects, and the environment. Fine motor development is related to the ability to draw, write, and participate in routines such as eating and dressing.

Beginning level: Children exhibit beginning responses. For instance, they hold hands in a fisted position or curl fingers around an adult's finger when it is placed in their palm.

Next level: Children reach for and grasp things and use eyes and hands to explore objects actively in the environment. For example, they keep hands open most of the time, or they may curl fingers and pull an object closer in a raking motion.

Next level: Children use full hand grasp with the thumb closed on the fist. For instance, they hold a crayon with a full fist, or they may adjust their grasp to the size and shape of a toy or food.

Next level: Children pick up or hold things with fingertip(s) and thumb. For example, they may hold a spoon, using thumb and fingers, to feed a doll; or they may use the index finger and thumb to pick up a piece of food.

Next level: Children manipulate objects using the fingers and wrist of one hand while stabilizing the object with the other hand. For instance, a child may use a turning motion with the hand and wrist while trying to open twist tops, or he may feed himself with one hand while stabilizing the dish with the other hand.

Next level: Children manipulate objects using the fingers and wrists of both hands together to accomplish a task or participate in an activity. For example, they can use child-safe scissors in one hand to make snips in a piece of paper, or they can string large wooden beads onto a shoelace.

Gross Motor

Definition: Gross motor development includes the attainment of skills such as rolling over, sitting up, crawling, walking, and running. Gross motor behavior enables children to move and thereby attain different perspectives on the environment. The gross motor behaviors involved in active outdoor play with other children are related to children's development of social skills and an understanding of social rules.

Beginning level: Children move their bodies with beginning responses or rudimentary responses. For instance, a child will move her legs or turn her head.

Next level: Children combine the movements of more than one body part. For example, they wave their arms and kick their legs at the same time, or they hold onto a foot while lying on their back.

Next level: Children coordinate movements of their arms and legs to move the whole body. For instance, they roll from stomach to back or from back to stomach; they move from lying down to a sitting position; or they move from a sitting position onto hands and knees.

Next level: Children coordinate movement of the whole body while using support to stand on two feet. For example, a child may use a table to pull himself to a standing position, or he may hold onto the table and side-step around it.

Next level: Children coordinate movement of the whole body while standing on two feet without support. For instance, they may squat to reach for a toy and stand up unassisted, or walk up stairs by putting two feet on a step before going to the next one.

Next level: Children coordinate highly complex movements with confidence and ease. For example, they may walk up steps, alternating their feet; walk on tiptoes; or run while holding a toy.

Engaging Families

By learning how to observe and facilitate children's perceptual and motor development, families gain a greater understanding of the connection between this domain and the other developmental domains. Infant

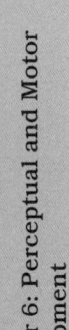

care teachers can play an important role in fostering an understanding of perceptual and motor development by engaging family members in conversation about this developmental domain, by sharing with families ideas for enjoying physical activities with their children, and by developing or identifying resources in the community that support young children's perceptual and motor development. It is also helpful to talk with families about how to plan experiences or provide simple materials at home that address all aspects of their children's perceptual and motor development. For example:

- Talk with families about how gross motor activities are not limited to parks and playgrounds, which may or may not be accessible to all families. An example of a fun activity that supports gross motor development is "painting" a sidewalk or fence using paintbrushes and rollers that have been dipped in water. Similarly, a walk in the neighborhood can provide opportunities to practice balancing, jumping, bending, and running.

- Suggest to families ways in which toddlers can engage in fine motor activities at home, such as by helping to sort blueberries or beans during meal preparation.

- Invite families to share songs, games, or other early childhood rituals that incorporate perceptual and motor development, and include some of those activities regularly in the early education setting. A few examples are songs and movements that young infants participate in while being held on someone's lap.

- Encourage families to take advantage of community resources (e.g., inclusive playgrounds) designed to support the perceptual and motor development of all children.

Questions for Reflection

1. What are some ways in which you can support the perceptual and motor development of all children, including those with special needs? How can you help the families of children with special needs to support their children's perceptual and motor development at home and in the community?

2. What are some ways you can use the information in the infant/toddler learning and development foundations and the infant/toddler curriculum framework to gain a deeper understanding and become a more careful observer of children's perceptual and

motor development? How would a deeper understanding of this developmental domain influence the ways in which you plan curriculum and partner with families?

Concluding Thoughts

The perceptual and motor development of infants and toddlers occurs within the broad context of overall development. With each new competency gained, the child's perceptual and motor behavior is developing hand in hand with his or her interpersonal orientation and social environment. As infants and toddlers are developing in all domains, they spend a significant part of each day engaged in a variety of motor behaviors. In light of children's active engagement in perceptual and motor learning, teachers need to keep overall development in mind while planning to support the children's ongoing processing of sensory information and fine and gross motor movements.

It is noteworthy that perceptual and motor development occurs in the context of culture, emotions, social relationships, and experience. The biological makeup and the sociocultural experiences of children blend together in unique ways. Indeed, though most children attain the same major motor milestones, each may follow a distinct developmental pathway. Teachers need to get to know every child well and adapt accordingly—both in the way they interact with the child and by setting up an appropriately challenging environment.

Recognizing perceptual and motor development in infants and toddlers and communicating with the children about that development are important. An observant teacher conveys interest in each child's drive to explore sensory and motor experiences and to attempt physically challenging movements. Responsiveness from teachers with whom infants have close relationships encourages the infants' continued exploration and movement. In addition, by describing children's actions, teachers can help children connect words with physical sensations and movement. This practice supports perceptual and motor development and facilitates the development of concepts and language. Finally, when teachers acknowledge an infant's or toddler's accomplishments, they send the message that they share in the child's pride of accomplishment, affirm the child's developing self-confidence, and deepen their relationship with the child.

Map of the Foundations

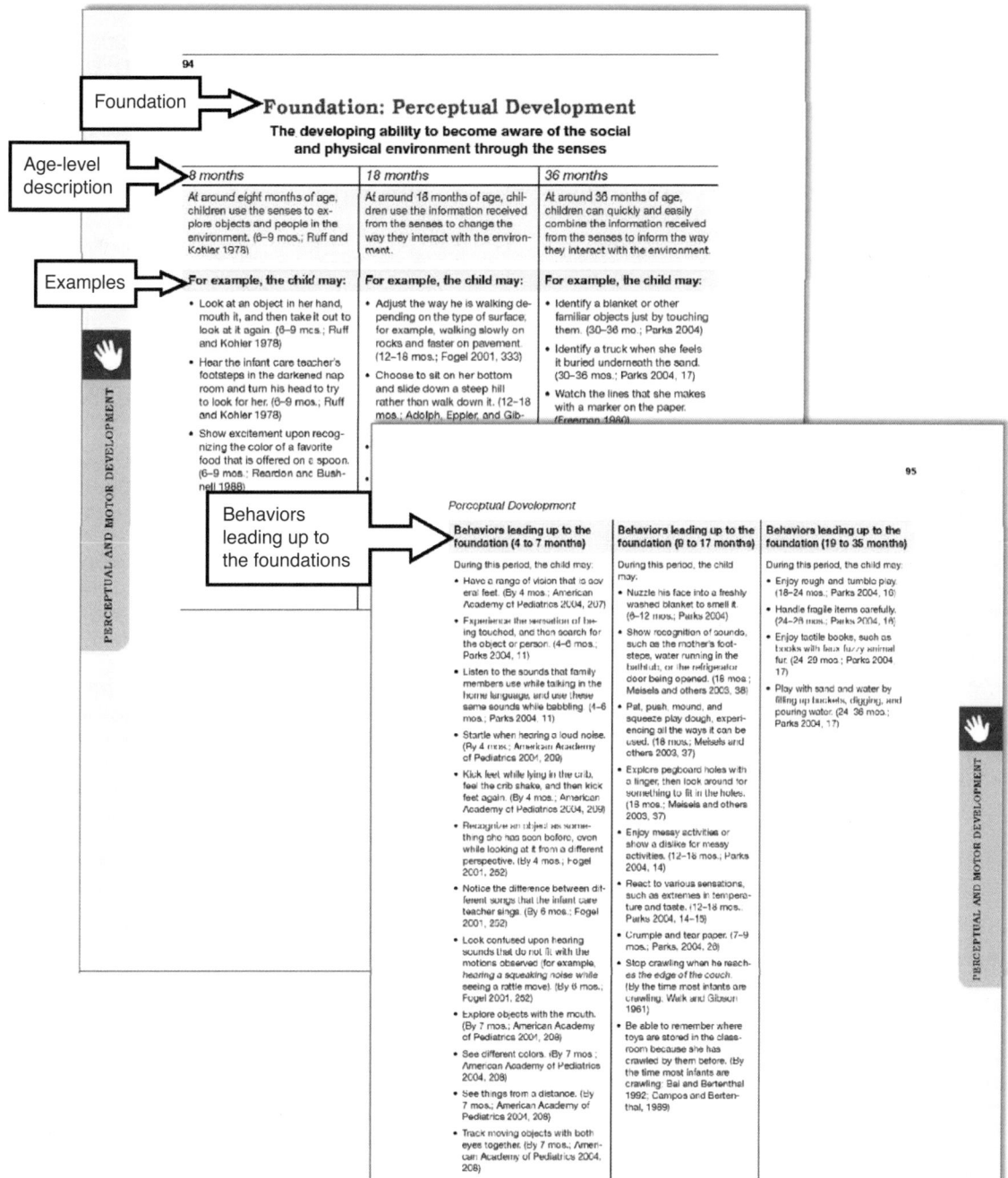

Teacher Resources

Body, Mind and Child. Web site. http://www.bodymindandchild.com/ (accessed September 7, 2010).

Ciervo, A. L., and C. Lerner. *Getting in Tune: The Powerful Influence of Music on Young Children's Development.* Baltimore, MD: Zero to Three, 2002.

Copple, C., and S. Bredekamp, eds. *Developmentally Appropriate Practice in Early Childhood Programs: Serving Children from Birth Through Age 8.* 3rd ed. Washington, DC: National Association for the Education of Young Children, 2009.

Dombro, A. L., L. J. Colker, and D. T. Dodge. *The Creative Curriculum for Infants and Toddlers.* Rev. ed. Washington, DC: Teaching Strategies, Inc., 1999.

Fernie, D. "The Nature of Children's Play." KidSource Online. http://www.kidsource.com/kidsource/content2/Nature.of.Childs.play.html (accessed September 7, 2010).

Lerner, C., and L. A. Ciervo. *Getting Ready for School Starts at Birth: How to Help Your Child Learn in the Early Years.* Brochure. Washington, DC: Zero to Three, 2004.

Lerner, C., and S. Greenip. *The Power of Play: Learning Through Play from Birth to Three.* Brochure. Washington, DC: Zero to Three, 2004.

McHenry, J. D., and K. J. Buerk. "Infants and Toddlers Meet the Natural World." *Young Children* 63, no.1 (January 2008): 40–41.

Nunley, K. Brains.org: Practical Classroom Applications of Current Brain Research. Web site. http://www.brains.org/ (accessed September 7, 2010).

Petersen, S. H., and D. S. Wittmer. *Endless Opportunities for Infant and Toddler Curriculum: A Relationship-Based Approach.* Upper Saddle River, NJ: Pearson Education, Inc., 2009.

Piaget, J. *The Origins of Intelligence in Children.* New York: International Universities Press, 1952.

Pica, R. *Experiences in Movement and Music: Birth to Age 8.* 4th ed. Belmont, CA: Cengage Learning, 2004.

———. *Moving and Learning Series: Toddlers.* Clifton Park, NY: Delmar Learning, 2000.

———. *Wiggle, Giggle, and Shake: 200 Ways to Move and Learn.* Beltsville, MD: Gryphon House, Inc., 2001.

Poest, C. A., and L. Leszynski. *Kinderkicks: Preschool Exercise and Nutrition.* Unpublished manuscript, 1988.

Poest, C. A., and others. "Challenge Me to Move: Large Muscle Development in Young Children." *Young Children* 45, no. 5 (July 1990): 4–10.

Project Zero: Harvard Graduate School of Education. Web site. http://www.pzweb.harvard.edu (accessed September 7, 2010).

Reiff, J. C. *Learning Styles: What Research Says to the Teacher* (series). Washington, DC: National Education Association, 1992.

Strickland, E. "Let's Go Outside." Scholastic, Inc. http://www.scholastic.com/resources/article/lets-go-outside (accessed November 22, 2011).

Swim, T. J., and L. Watson. *Infants and Toddlers: Curriculum and Teaching.* 6th ed. Belmont, CA: Cengage Learning, 2008.

Taras, H. L. "Physical Activity of Young Children in Relation to Physical and Mental Health," in *Young Children on the Grow: Health, Activity, and Education in the Preschool Setting.* Edited by C. M. Hendricks. Teacher Education Monograph no. 13. Washington, DC: Eric Clearinghouse on Teacher Education, 1992.

Tortora, S., C. Lerner, and L. Ciervo. *On the Move: The Power of Movement in Your Child's First Three Years.* Brochure. Washington, DC: Zero to Three, 2004.

U.S. Department of Health and Human Services, Administration for Children and Families (ACF), Office of Child Care (OCC), National Child Care Information and Technical Assistance Center (NCCIC). Web site. http://nccic.acf.hhs.gov/ (accessed November 22, 2011).

Williams, H. G. *Perceptual and Motor Development.* Englewood Cliffs, NJ: Prentice-Hall, 1983.

Williamson, G. G., and M. E. Anzalone. *Sensory Integration and Self-Regulation in Infants and Toddlers: Helping Very Young Children Interact with Their Environment.* Washington, DC: Zero to Three, 2001.

Endnotes

1. B. I. Bertenthal, "Origins and Early Development of Perception, Action and Representation," *Annual Review of Psychology* 47 (1996): 431–59.

2. L. E. Bahrick, R. Lickliter, and R. Flom, "Intersensory Redundancy Guides the Development of Selective Attention, Perception, and Cognition in Infancy," *Current Directions in Psychological Science* 13, no. 3 (2004): 99–102.

3. K. E. Adolph, I. Weise, and L. Marin, "Motor Development," in *Encyclopedia of Cognitive Science* (London: Macmillan, 2003), p. 134.

4. K. E. Adolph, "Learning in the Development of Infant Locomotion," *Monographs of the Society for Research in Child Development* 62, serial no. 251, no. 3 (1997): 52–53.

5. K. E. Adolph and A. S. Joh, "Motor Development: How Infants Get Into the Act," in *Introduction to Infant Development,* 2nd ed. Edited by A. Slater and M. Lewis (New York: Oxford University Press, 2007).

6. K. E. Adolph, "Learning in the Development of Infant Locomotion," *Monographs of the Society for Research in Child Development* 62, serial no. 251, no. 3 (1997): 4.

7. K. E. Adolph and S. E. Berger, "Motor Development," in *Handbook of Child Psychology, Volume 2: Cognition, Perception, and Language,* 6th ed., series edited by W. Damon and R. M. Lerner, volume edited by D. Kuhn and R. Siegler (Hoboken, NJ: John Wiley and Sons, 2006).

8. K. E. Adolph and A. M. Avolio, "Walking Infants Adapt Locomotion to Changing Body Dimensions," *Journal of Experimental Psychology: Human Perception and Performance* 26, no. 3 (2000): 1148.

9. K. E. Adolph and S. E. Berger, "Motor Development," in *Handbook of Child Psychology, Volume 2: Cognition, Perception, and Language,* 6th ed., series edited by W. Damon and R. M. Lerner, volume edited by D. Kuhn and R. Siegler (Hoboken, NJ: John Wiley and Sons, 2006).

10. M. M. Haith, C. Hazen, and G. S. Goodman, "Expectation and Anticipation of Dynamic Visual Events by 3.5 Month-Old Babies," *Child Development* 59, no. 2 (1988): 467–79.

11. K. E. Adolph and A. S. Joh, "Motor Development: How Infants Get Into the Act," in *Introduction to Infant Development,* 2nd ed., edited by A. Slater and M. Lewis (New York: Oxford University Press, 2007), p. 11.

12. K. E. Adolph and S. E. Berger, "Motor Development," in *Handbook of Child Psychology, Volume 2: Cognition, Perception, and Language,* 6th ed., series edited by W. Damon and R. M. Lerner, volume edited by D. Kuhn and R. Siegler (Hoboken, NJ: John Wiley and Sons, 2006), p. 181.

13. Ibid.

14. B. I. Bertenthal and S. M. Boker, "New Paradigms and New Issues: A Comment on Emerging Themes in the Study of Motor Development," *Monographs of the Society for Research in Child Development* 62, no. 3 (1997): 141–51.

15. E. W. Bushnell and J. P. Boudreau, "Motor Development and the Mind: the Potential Role of Motor Abilities as a Determinant of Aspects of Perceptual Development," *Child Development* 64, no. 4 (1993): 1005–21.

16. H. L. Pick, "Motor Development: The Control of Action," *Developmental Psychology* 25, no. 6 (1989): 867–70.

17. Ibid.

18. B. I. Bertenthal, "Origins and Early Development of Perception, Action and Representation," *Annual Review of Psychology* 47 (1996): 431–59.

19. E. J. Gibson, "Exploratory Behavior in the Development of Perceiving, Acting and the Acquiring of Knowledge," *Annual Review of Psychology* 39, no. 1 (1988): 4.

20. E. Thelen, "Motor Development: A New Synthesis," *American Psychologist* 50, no. 2 (1995): 79–95.

21. E. J. Gibson, "Exploratory Behavior in the Development of Perceiving, Acting and the Acquiring of Knowledge," *Annual Review of Psychology* 39, no. 1 (1988): 4–5.

22. E. Thelen, "Motor Development: A New Synthesis," *American Psychologist* 50, no. 2 (1995): 79–95.

23. C. Von Hofsten, "Action in Development," *Developmental Science* 10, no. 1 (2007): 54–60.

24. K. E. Adolph and S. E. Berger, "Physical and Motor Development," in *Developmental Science: An Advanced Textbook*, 5th ed., edited by M. H. Bornstein and M. E. Lamb (Hillsdale, NJ: Lawrence Erlbaum Associates, 2005).

25. K. E. Adolph, "Motor and Physical Development: Locomotion," in *Encyclopedia of Infant and Early Childhood Development*, edited by M. M. Haith and J. B. Benson (San Diego, CA: Academic Press, 2008).

26. Ibid.

27. K. E. Adolph, I. Weise, and L. Marin, "Motor Development," in *Encyclopedia of Cognitive Science* (London: Macmillan, 2003).

28. K. E. Adolph, "Learning in the Development of Infant Locomotion," *Monographs of the Society for Research in Child Development* 62, serial no. 251, no. 3 (1997): 99–106.

29. K. E. Adolph, "Motor and Physical Development: Locomotion," in *Encyclopedia of Infant and Early Childhood Development*, edited by M. M. Haith and J. B. Benson (San Diego, CA: Academic Press, 2008).

30. K. E. Adolph and A. S. Joh, "Motor Development: How Infants Get Into the Act," in *Introduction to Infant Development*, 2nd ed., edited by A. Slater and M. Lewis (New York: Oxford University Press, 2007).

31. K. E. Adolph, "Motor and Physical Development: Locomotion," in *Encyclopedia of Infant and Early Childhood Development*, edited by M. M. Haith and J. B. Benson (San Diego, CA: Academic Press, 2008).

32. Ibid.

33. K. E. Adolph and A. S. Joh, "Motor Development: How Infants Get Into the Act," in *Introduction to Infant Development*, 2nd ed., edited by A. Slater and M. Lewis (New York: Oxford University Press, 2007).

34. K. E. Adolph, B. Vereijken, and P. E. Shrout, "What Changes in Infant Walking and Why," *Child Development* 74, no. 2 (2003): 475–97.

35. K. E. Adolph and S. E. Berger, "Motor Development," in *Handbook of Child Psychology, Volume 2: Cognition, Perception, and Language*, 6th ed., series edited by W. Damon and R. M. Lerner, volume edited by D. Kuhn and R. Siegler (Hoboken, NJ: John Wiley and Sons, 2006), p. 173.

36. E. Thelen, "Motor Development: A New Synthesis," *American Psychologist* 50, no. 2 (1995): 79–95.

37. E. Thelen, "Three-Month-Old Infants Can Learn Task-Specific Patterns of Interlimb Coordination," *Psychological Science* 5, no. 5 (1994): 280–85.

38. K. E. Adolph and S. E. Berger, "Physical and Motor Development," in *Developmental Science: An Advanced Textbook*, 5th ed., edited by M. H. Bornstein and M. E. Lamb (Hillsdale, NJ: Lawrence Erlbaum Associates, 2005).

39. A. Diamond, "Interrelated and Interdependent," *Developmental Science* 10, no. 1 (2007): 152–58.

40. Ibid.

41. Ibid.

42. B. I. Bertenthal, "Origins and Early Development of Perception, Action and Representation," *Annual Review of Psychology* 47 (1996): 431–59.

43. E. J. Gibson, "What Does Infant Perception Tell Us About Theories of Perception?," *Journal of Experimental Psychology: Human Perception and Performance* 13, no. 4 (1987): 515–23.

44. E. J. Gibson, "Exploratory Behavior in the Development of Perceiving, Acting and the Acquiring of Knowledge," *Annual Review of Psychology* 39, no. 1 (1988): 5.

45. N. E. Berthier, "Learning to Reach: A Mathematical Model," *Developmental Psychology* 32, no. 5 (1996): 811.

46. E. Thelen, "Motor Development: A New Synthesis," *American Psychologist* 50, no. 2 (1995): 79–95.

47. K. E. Adolph and S. E. Berger, "Physical and Motor Development," in *Developmental Science: An Advanced Textbook*, 5th ed., edited by M. H. Bornstein and M. E. Lamb (Hillsdale, NJ: Lawrence Erlbaum Associates, 2005), p. 223.

48. C. S. Tamis-LeMonda and K. E. Adolph, "Social Referencing in Infant Motor Action," in *The Development of Social Cognition and Communication*, edited by B. D. Homer and C. S. Tamis-LeMonda (Mahwah, NJ: Lawrence Erlbaum Associates, 2005).

49. J. Gonzalez-Mena and D. W. Eyer, *Infants, Toddlers, and Caregivers: A Curriculum of Respectful, Responsive Care and Education*, 6th ed. (New York: McGraw-Hill Companies, 2003), p. 129.

50. M. Gerber, *Dear Parent: Caring for Infants and Toddlers with Respect*, 2nd ed., edited by J. Weaver (Los Angeles: Resources for Infant Educators [RIE], 2001), p. 19.

51. K. E. Adolph and S. E. Berger, "Motor Development," in *Handbook of Child Psychology, Volume 2: Cognition, Perception, and Language*, 6th ed., series edited by W. Damon and R. M. Lerner, volume edited by D. Kuhn and R. Siegler (Hoboken, NJ: John Wiley and Sons, 2006), p. 173.

52. K. E. Adolph, "Learning in the Development of Infant Locomotion," *Monographs of the Society for Research in Child Development* 62, serial no. 251, no. 3 (1997): 12–14.

53. L. J. Claxton, R. Keen, and M. E. McCarty, "Evidence of Motor Planning in Infant Reaching Behavior," *Psychological Science* 14, no. 4 (2003): 354–56.

54. Ibid.

Bibliography

Adolph, K. E. "Learning in the Development of Infant Locomotion." *Monographs of the Society for Research in Child Development* 62, serial no. 251, no. 3 (1997): 1–164.

———. "Motor and Physical Development: Locomotion," in *Encyclopedia of Infant and Early Childhood Development*. Edited by M. M. Haith and J. B. Benson. San Diego, CA: Academic Press, 2008.

Adolph, K. E., and A. M. Avolio. "Walking Infants Adapt Locomotion to Changing Body Dimensions." *Journal of Experimental Psychology: Human Perception and Performance* 26, no. 3 (2000): 1148–66.

Adolph, K. E., and S. E. Berger. "Motor Development," in *Handbook of Child Psychology, Volume 2: Cognition, Perception, and Language*. 6th ed. Series edited by W. Damon and R. M. Lerner, volume edited D. Kuhn and R. Siegler. Hoboken, NJ: John Wiley and Sons, 2006.

———. "Physical and Motor Development," in *Developmental Science: An Advanced Textbook*. 5th ed. Edited by M. H. Bornstein and M. E. Lamb. Hillsdale, NJ: Lawrence Erlbaum Associates, 2005.

Adolph, K. E., and A. S. Joh. "Motor Development: How Infants Get Into the Act," in *Introduction to Infant Development*. 2nd ed. Edited by A. Slater and M. Lewis. New York: Oxford University Press, 2007.

Adolph, K. E., B. Vereijken, and P. E. Shrout. "What Changes in Infant Walking and Why." *Child Development* 74, no. 2 (2003): 5–97.

Adolph, K. E., I. Weise, and L. Marin. "Motor Development," in *Encyclopedia of Cognitive Science*. London: Macmillan, 2003.

Bahrick, L. E., R. Lickliter, and R. Flom. "Intersensory Redundancy Guides the Development of Selective Attention, Perception, and Cognition in Infancy." *Current Directions in Psychological Science* 13, no. 3 (2004): 99–102.

Bertenthal, B. I. "Origins and Early Development of Perception, Action and Representation." *Annual Review of Psychology* 47 (1996): 431–59.

Bertenthal, B. I., and S. M. Boker. "New Paradigms and New Issues: A Comment on Emerging Themes in the Study of Motor Development." *Monographs of the Society*

for Research in Child Development 62, no. 3 (1997): 141–51.

Berthier, N. E. "Learning to Reach: A Mathematical Model." *Developmental Psychology* 32, no. 5 (1996): 811–23.

Bushnell, E. W., and J. P. Boudreau. "Motor Development and the Mind: the Potential Role of Motor Abilities as a Determinant of Aspects of Perceptual Development." *Child Development* 64, no. 4 (1993): 1005–21.

Claxton, L. J., R. Keen, and M. E. McCarty. "Evidence of Motor Planning in Infant Reaching Behavior." *Psychological Science* 14, no. 4 (2003): 354–56.

Diamond, A. "Interrelated and Interdependent." *Developmental Science* 10, no. 1 (2007): 152–58.

Gerber, M. *Dear Parent: Caring for Infants and Toddlers with Respect.* 2nd ed. Edited by J. Weaver. Los Angeles: Resources for Infant Educators (RIE), 2001.

Gibson, E. J. "Exploratory Behavior in the Development of Perceiving, Acting and the Acquiring of Knowledge." *Annual Review of Psychology* 39, no. 1 (1988): 1–41.

———. "What Does Infant Perception Tell Us About Theories of Perception?" *Journal of Experimental Psychology: Human Perception and Performance* 13, no. 4 (1987): 515–23.

Gonzalez–Mena, J., and D. W. Eyer. *Infants, Toddlers, and Caregivers: A Curriculum of Respectful, Responsive Care and Education.* 6th ed. New York: McGraw-Hill Companies, 2003.

Haith, M. M., C. Hazen, and G. S. Goodman. "Expectation and Anticipation of Dynamic Visual Events by 3.5 Month-Old Babies." *Child Development* 59, no. 2 (1988): 467–79.

Pick, H. L. "Motor Development: The Control of Action." *Developmental Psychology* 25, no. 6 (1989): 867–70.

Tamis-LeMonda, C. S., and K. E. Adolph. "Social Referencing in Infant Motor Action," in *The Development of Social Cognition and Communication.* Edited by B. D. Homer and C. S. Tamis-LeMonda. Mahwah, NJ: Lawrence Erlbaum Associates, 2005.

Thelen, E. "Motor Development: A New Synthesis." *American Psychologist* 50, no. 2 (1995): 79–95.

———. "Three-Month-Old Infants Can Learn Task-Specific Patterns of Interlimb Coordination." *Psychological Science* 5, no. 5 (1994): 280–85.

Von Hofsten, C. "Action in Development." *Developmental Science* 10, no. 1 (2007): 54–60.

Appendix

Resources for Teachers of Children with Disabilities or Other Special Needs

***Achieving Learning Goals Through Play: Teaching Young Children with Special Needs* (2nd ed.).** Author: A. H. Widerstrom. Baltimore, MD: Brookes Publishing Company, 2004. http://brookespublishing.com/store/books/widerstrom-6989/index.htm (accessed January 18, 2012).

Play is more than just fun; it is a powerful teaching tool that helps young children learn. This guide provides ready-to-use strategies for weaving individual learning goals into play throughout the school day. It was created for use with children from ages two through five who have special needs, but it is equally effective for typically developing children. The book includes information on how play activities can help children develop cognitive, communication, motor, social, and preliteracy skills. The appendixes offer guidelines for developmentally appropriate practice, resources for including children with disabilities, and reproducible planning matrixes.

***Adapting Early Childhood Curricula for Children with Special Needs* (7th ed.).** Authors: R. E. Cook, M. D. Klein, and A. Tessier. Upper Saddle River, NJ: Merrill, 2007. http://pearsonhighered.com/educator/product/Adapting-Early-Childhood-Curricula-for-Children-with-Special-Needs/9780131723818.page (accessed January 18, 2012).

This book takes a practical, "activity-based" approach that is theoretically sound and current. It also discusses specific intervention strategies that enhance teachers' use of embedded learning opportunities within daily curriculum activities and routines. The content is relatively jargon-free and is built on evidence-based practices, making it appropriate for a wide range of readers. Illustrations of techniques and strategies make it a useful resource that promotes an inclusive, family-centered approach to working with young children with special needs and their families.

Building Strong Foundations. Authors: R. Parlakian and N. L. Seibel. Washington, DC: Zero to Three, 2002. https://secure2.convio.net/zttcfn/site/Ecommerce/1638030496?VIEW_PRODUCT=true&product_id=1761&store_id=1121 (accessed January 18, 2012).

This publication explores the ways in which supportive relationships at all levels of an infant care program—between supervisor and staff members, staff members and families, parents and children—contribute to children's healthy social–emotional development, which is sometimes referred to as "infant mental health." The authors present the core concepts of infant mental health, offer strategies for leaders and trainers on how to promote children's mental health, and describe guidelines on when to refer very young children for assessment and treatment. To bring concepts to life, the book includes numerous vignettes featuring a mix of infant/family settings. Exercises designed to help staff and leaders better understand and apply infant mental health practices are also included.

California Map to Inclusion & Belonging. http://cainclusion.org/camap/ (accessed January 18, 2012).

The California Map to Inclusion & Belonging Web site, operated by the WestEd Center for Child and Family Studies and funded by the California Department of Education's Child Development Division (with a portion of the federal Child Care Development Fund Quality Improvement Allocation), offers many resources and Web links to support children with special needs and their families.

DEC Recommended Practices: A Comprehensive Guide for Practical Application in Early Intervention/ Early Childhood Special Education. Authors: S. R. Sandall and others. Missoula, MT: The Division for Early Childhood (DEC), 2005. http://www.dec-sped.org/Store/Recommended Practices (accessed January 18, 2012).

In addition to providing all of the information from the original *DEC Recommended Practices,* this guide offers real-life examples and practical tips for implementation. The book includes strategies for assessing and improving programs, checklists for parents and administrators, and an annotated list of relevant resources.

The Exceptional Child: Inclusion in Early Childhood Education (6th ed.). Authors: E. K. Allen and G. E. Cowdery. Florence, KY: Cengage Learning, 2008. http://www.cengage.com/search/productOverview.do?Ntt=Allen||9781418074012&Ntk=all||P_Isbn13&Ns=P_Product_Title&N=0 (accessed January 18, 2012).

This book presents history and research on the legal issues, disabilities, and other considerations that are relevant to educating children with special needs. It addresses the approach and tools needed to provide an optimal setting for the children and their families. The publication includes forms and checklists that educators can use in the classroom to create developmentally appropriate environments. Its easy-to-use format was designed to assist educators, care providers, and parents.

Inclusion Works! Creating Child Care Programs That Promote Belonging for Children with Special Needs. Author: California Department of Education. Sacramento: California Department of Education, 2009. http://www.cde.ca.gov/re/pn/rc/ap/pubdisplay.aspx?ID=001689 (accessed January 18, 2012).

This publication offers guidance and proven strategies that promote belonging and inclusion for all children. Building on research and the experience gained from years of effective implementation, the book includes stories, examples, background information, and resources that support successful inclusive practices. Suggestions for ways to adapt the environment are provided, along with examples of inclusive strategies. A glossary and appendixes make this handbook a practical tool for care providers.

Inclusive Child Care for Infants and Toddlers: Meeting Individual and Special Needs. Author: M. O'Brien. Baltimore, MD: Brookes Publishing Company, 1997. http://www.brookespublishing.com/store/books/obrien-2967/index.htm (accessed January 18, 2012).

This book presents child care providers with advice on handling daily caregiving tasks, teaching responsively, meeting individual needs, developing rapport with parents, understanding toddlers' behavior, working with Individualized Family Service Plans, and maintaining high standards of care. Suggested play activities and intervention approaches help promote healthy development in all children. The publication also includes checklists for assessing quality, parent report forms, and feeding/play schedules that target developing skills in areas in which infants and toddlers need the most help.

Inclusive Early Childhood Education: Development, Resources, and Practice (5th ed.). Author: P. L. Deiner. Florence, KY: Cengage Learning, 2010. http://www.cengage.com/search/productOverview.do?N=+11&Ntk=P_Isbn13&Ntt=9781428320864 (accessed January 18, 2012).

This comprehensive special education resource was designed to help early childhood educators with the diagnosis and education of children who have a variety of learning disabilities. The text includes extensive coverage of disabilities—comparable to the content of many "Introduction to Special Education" courses. The book also offers guidelines, vignettes, and hands-on program planning to prepare educators to integrate children with learning disabilities into regular classroom instruction.

Mental Health Consultation in Child Care. Authors: K. Johnston and C. Brinamen. Washington, DC: Zero to Three, 2006. https://secure2.convio.net/zttcfn/site/Ecommerce/1638030496?VIEW_PRODUCT=true&product_id=1301&store_id=1121 (accessed January 18, 2012).

As young children spend more time in child care programs, those programs have an increasingly significant effect on children's social and emotional development. This book discusses the impact of the caregiver–child relationship on the mental health of young children. It reviews current theory and offers practical suggestions for improving relationships among program directors, staff members, parents, children, and mental health consultants. The book aims to help mental health professionals, early childhood educators and trainers, and policymakers identify and remove obstacles to quality care and make positive changes in child care environments.

Mental Health in Early Intervention: Achieving Unity in Principles and Practice. Edited by G. M. Foley and J. D. Hochman. Baltimore, MD: Brookes Publishing Company, 2006. http://www.brookespublishing.com/store/books/foley-7381/index.htm (accessed January 18, 2012).

Too often, infant mental health and early intervention are dealt with separately rather than together. Integration of these two interdependent fields is the goal of this publication. The book prepares readers to combine the two fields and improve practices in both.

Sensory Integration and Self-Regulation in Infants and Toddlers: Helping Very Young Children Interact with Their Environment. Authors: G. G. Williamson and M. E. Anzalone. Washington, DC: Zero to Three, 2001. https://secure2.convio.net/zttcfn/site/Ecommerce/1648541119?VIEW_PRODUCT=true&product_id=1041&store_id=1121 (accessed January 18, 2012).

This book was written for an audience of multidisciplinary practitioners who support the development of infants and young children in a broad range of settings—including child care, Head Start and Early Head Start, early intervention, neonatal intensive care follow-up, developmental clinics, infant mental health centers, and child life programs. The authors integrate and synthesize knowledge from the fields of occupational therapy, neuroscience, child development, psychology, psychiatry, education, and the movement sciences to help readers understand the sensory development of infants and young children; learn about assessment and intervention approaches designed to promote very young children's self-regulation and adaptive behavior; and gain awareness of new directions and questions in basic and applied research in the field.

Social and Emotional Health in Early Childhood: Building Bridges Between Services and Systems. Edited by D. F. Perry, R. K. Kaufmann, and J. Knitzer. Baltimore, MD: Brookes Publishing Company, 2007. http://www.brookespublishing.com/store/books/perry-67823/index.htm (accessed January 18, 2012).

Social and emotional health are critical factors in a child's development and school readiness—factors that depend on weaving effective mental health services into other systems and programs that support young children. This publication will help professionals discover how to improve young children's outcomes by building sturdy bridges between mental health services and medical, educational, and social services. Brief stories throughout the book illustrate how mental health services help children and families at risk. Two real-life case studies give readers an inside look at effective early childhood mental health systems, including structure, financing, and evaluation of outcomes.

Social Competence of Young Children: Risk, Disability, and Intervention. Edited by W. H. Brown, S. L. Odom, and S. R. McConnell. Baltimore, MD: Brookes Publishing Company, 2007. http://www.brookespublishing.com/store/books/brown-69230/index.htm (accessed January 18, 2012).

Increasing positive peer interaction can reduce future social competence problems, but how can you ensure that children with developmental difficulties are given a chance to cultivate the social relationships they need? This book details current, research-based assessment and intervention strategies, along with well-matched and effective peer interaction interventions—classroom, naturalistic, or explicit—to suit specific children's needs.

Teaching Infants, Toddlers, and Twos with Special Needs. Author: C. Willis. Baltimore, MD: Gryphon House, 2009. http://www.gryphonhouse.com/store/trans/productDetailForm.asp?CatID=26&BookID=15089 (accessed January 18, 2012).

Placing children with special needs in environments that include typically developing peers has become commonplace, as research continues to confirm that all children benefit and learn from each other and from their teachers. This book was written for all teachers and directors who work with infants and toddlers, including special education professionals and educators who work with typically developing children. It focuses on the needs of children with developmental delays and on children who are at risk of developing special needs. Each chapter includes information on how young children learn, as well as strategies and adaptations that apply to all children. Examples are presented for managing the physical environment and for teaching skills that will enhance the overall development of infants and toddlers with special needs.

Young Children with Disabilities in Natural Environments: Methods and Procedures. Authors: M. J. Noonan and L. McCormick. Baltimore, MD: Brookes Publishing Company, 2006. http://brookespublishing.com/store/books/noonan-8612/index.htm (accessed January 18, 2012).

Focusing on children from birth to age five who have disabilities, this publication provides specific, practical knowledge on how to work effectively with children in natural environments. It includes clear methods; an integrated approach that blends information from different disabilities, developmental domains, and ages; and a strong focus on cultural competence.